CREATIVE COMMUNION

Toward a Spirituality
of Work

Joe Holland

PAULIST PRESS
New York / Mahwah, N.J.

Library of Congress Cataloging-in-Publication Data

Holland, Joe.
 Creative communion: toward a spirituality of work/Joe Holland.
  p. cm.
 Bibliography: p.
 ISBN 0-8091-3046-7 (pbk.): $5.95 (est.)
 1. Work—Religious aspects—Catholic Church. 2. Economics—Re-
ligious aspects—Catholic Church. 3. Catholic Church—Doctrines.
I. Title
BT738.5.H65 1989
261.8'5—dc19   88-29115
                   CIP

Published by Paulist Press
997 Macarthur Boulevard
Mahwah, N.J. 07430

Printed and bound in the
United States of America

Contents

Introduction: The Work Crisis of Modern Culture   1

1. The Modern Degradation of Work   7

2. Work as Co-Creation   18

3. Toward a Holistic Economy   43

4. Post-Modern Pastoral Implications   68

Notes   84

*For creative leaders of community
across the global labor movement
north and south, east and west*

Introduction:
The Work Crisis
of Modern Culture

A Personal Journey

The publication of this small book grows from a major shift in my theological focus. It is a shift from concern with the political economy to concern with culture and spirituality. My exploration of culture and spirituality is from a Catholic perspective, but hopefully it will both serve the Catholic tradition and have wider uses.

I do not see this shift in focus from the political-economic region to the cultural-spiritual region as a break, but rather as a deepening. Still perceiving the political economy as providing the fundamental social structures to contextualize our religious experience, I have nonetheless made the judgment that the key to the meaning and energy of these structures is to be found in spirituality and culture. (I understand spirituality to be the depth of culture and culture to be the wider expression of an implicit spirituality.) Hence the two apparently separate concerns are in my view two complementary sides of the same coin.[1]

1

As I turned to the spiritual-cultural region, a number of related proposals began to emerge in my imagination:

1. that we are entering the traumatic end of modern culture, and the diminishment of the cultural dualism so strong in the west since the time of classical Greece;

2. that in the midst of this crisis, we are seeing the emergence of the first seeds of a holistic, post-modern, ecologically-centered culture, reintegrating science and spirituality in a fresh cosmology, as revealed by sub-atomic and astro-physics through the use of computerized microscopic and telescopic technologies from the micro-electronic revolution;[2]

3. that this cultural turn is the key to interpreting the present crisis of American culture (the heart of modernity), with the consequent challenge of either creatively reconstructing American culture in dialogue with the holistic post-modern cosmology, or of retreating into a nostalgic, idolatrous, and finally destructive ideology of national security;

4. similarly that this cultural turn is also the key to the turbulence in contemporary Catholicism, with the most creative path pointing toward regeneration of a holistic, lay-centered church, while another path tempts the church to reassert classical dualistic categories in the name of ecclesial security;

5. that for American Catholicism the first step of prophetic creativity is the articulation of a lay spirituality, rooted in family and work, and interpreted within a dialogue between the Catholic tradition and the fresh cosmology.

This present work addresses the theme of work as one major pole of a lay spirituality shaped by the post-modern cosmology. The other major pole is family, which I plan to address in a future writing. Finally the entire framework of the spiritual-cultural transition will hopefully be the subject of still other writings.[3]

All that is proposed here remains at the level of intuition. I do not see it as my present task to argue or to prove these proposals, only to share them for wider reflection. My limited intention, therefore, is to unfold the intuition as a preface to more extensive testing in theory and practice.

Hopefully readers will excuse me if, in unfolding the intuition, I speak as if it were certain. That is a requirement of the genre. In the final analysis, what is here proposed may be true, or untrue, or partially true. But there seems no other way to unfold an intuition except by entering affirmatively into its vision. So I will speak from within the vision, but only to open a dialogue.

Spiritual Meaning of Work

For modern culture, the late twentieth century is a time of traumatic transformation. The two dominant modern ideologies, industrial capitalism and scientific socialism, are losing cultural energy. Pressed to their logical conclusions, they threaten the creative and communal fabric of our ecological, social, and spiritual life.

To counter the threats of these modern ideologies, a new cultural energy is arising. So profound is this new energy that it promises to create a fresh civilization. For lack of an agreed name, I call this new civilization the post-modern culture.[4]

At the heart of this new cultural energy is a religious renewal, in Catholicism as well as in other Christian streams and other world religions. For Catholicism, this religious renewal is increasingly lay-centered, creating a model of church which grows beyond the medieval higher/lower dualism and beyond the modern objective/subjective dualism, both of which have marginalized the laity and separated religious energies from ordinary life.

In this fresh lay-centered Catholic energy, a key theme is the spiritual meaning of work. A post-modern spirituality of work becomes a leading guide for Christians in the midst of the crisis of modern culture. Indeed, as already mentioned, a spirituality of work, along with a spirituality of family, is crucial for the creation of a post-modern lay-centered Christian spirituality of life.

Along with its divinely inspired technological development, modern culture has also been degrading work by organizing it more and more for the destruction of life. A fundamental task for post-modern civilization, and so for the renewal of Christianity, is to heal life by recovering the authentic meaning of work. In the post-modern cosmology, the religious imagination perceives work as human participation in the communion of life's ecological, social, and divine creativity.

Four Inter-Related Themes

In exploring this post-modern spirituality of work, I will address four inter-related themes, each in a separate but brief chapter.

The first theme (Chapter 1) is the modern degradation of work. Here we will look at how the energies of modern culture are degrading work and threatening the life system of our planet. This threat is seen as flowing from the modern mechanistic vision of science, and resulting in an inversion of the principle of the priority of labor.

The second theme (Chapter 2) is the post-modern spiritual vision of work as the co-creativity of ecological, social, and divine communion. In creative work we become co-creators with other humans, with nature, and through these two with God. But to understand this vision, we need first to lay bare the dualistic and reductionist interpretations of work which formerly functioned, perhaps for important purposes, in both western Christian classical and modern spiritualities and in the capitalist and communist ideologies of modernity.

The third theme (Chapter 3) is the structure and process

of a post-modern holistic economy, as it flows from the linkage of humanity's most primal mythic memories and the new micro-electronic technology. Seeds of such an economy are found in an artistic attitude toward life, in a recovery of our rootedness in nature, in the retrieval of primal community and the creation of global networking, in the cooperative organization of labor using appropriate technology, and in the recovery of the spiritual depths of economic creativity. Movement toward this economy in turn entails a recovery of the primal visions in Genesis and in Jesus' life and teaching.

The fourth theme (Chapter 4) is the pastoral implication of movement toward such a post-modern holistic or holy economy. These implications bear on issues like a pastoral consciousness of work, the post-modern model of family, the modern crisis of unemployment, and the culturally shifting role of unions.

Again, this is an exploratory reflection, in the manner of an unfolding intuition—all for further reflection and testing.

A Word of Thanks

I am very grateful to many people who helped me to understand the work crisis of modern culture, from both conservative and liberal viewpoints, and from the experience of religion and labor. They are so many, but I think especially of countless people in audiences around the world, for whom I was supposedly the teacher, but who by their questions and insight constantly taught me.

My special thanks to Mary Perkins Ryan and Ruth Coyne who helped a great deal in conceptualizing and editing this text. Thanks too to David Simons who brought it to the light of day after several years of dormancy.

1.
The Modern Degradation of Work

In this chapter, I will sketch a critique of the modern vision of work, and later in Chapter 2 sketch a related critique of classical and modern western spiritualities and of modern western ideologies. But these critiques need to be set in the context of appreciation for the extraordinary contributions of the modern technological awakening, itself a gift from God, and in the context of appreciation for the contributions of classical and modern western spiritualities, themselves a paradoxical key to the west's pioneering of technological consciousness.

The critiques may seem to suggest that it would have been better if these spiritualities and ideologies had not emerged. But that is not my view. The critique is not of these spiritualities or ideologies in their original context, but only as guides for our future.

In other words, my assumption is that the visions of these spiritualities and ideologies have outlived their usefulness as the dominant guides for our civilization. These spiritualities and ideologies have had their purpose as dominant shapers of the western tradition. Their contributions remain important. But now it may be time for the leadership of a different vision.

Modern Root Metaphor: The Machine

The crisis of late modern culture can be ultimately traced to its underlying imagination. Buried in the foundational imagination of every stage of human civilization is a single "root metaphor." This root metaphor shapes according to its image the culture's basic perception of ecological, social, and spiritual experience.[5]

The metaphor at the root of the modern imagination is the machine. So we speak of modern civilization as mechanistic. The modern understanding of science (which is only one model of science) is analytical. It sees all reality as something to be separated into its distinct parts, measured, weighed, and then organized into mass force—all like parts of a machine. For the mechanistic vision, the truth is in the separated parts. Hence we can say that modernity has been guided by a mechanistic vision of science.

This mechanistic vision comes to us from the foundational thinkers of the modern world, especially René Descartes in philosophy, Isaac Newton in physics, and Charles Darwin in biology. Similarly we might speak of John Locke for liberal politics and Adam Smith for liberal economics as seminal modern mechanistic thinkers.[6]

Within modern culture, work becomes the instrument of a great social machine of progress and freedom, organized according to the criteria of its mechanistic vision. In this vision, modern progress becomes a process of uprooting the future from the past, and modern freedom a structure of fragmentation where the whole is dissolved into its parts. As the modern mechanistic culture grows, the resulting social machine envelops more and more of our life.

Effects of Mechanization

Paradoxically as modern society advances, all life on earth seems threatened. Our ecological foundations begin to be undermined, threatened slowly by the ecological crisis, or rapidly by nuclear holocaust. In so many situations the social community, including family, erodes into atomized individualism. Even the spiritual depth of public culture is steadily flattened into a hollow meaninglessness.

Unfortunately the cultural root of this destructive pattern is embedded, like an expanding cancer, in the mechanistic organizational style of our most fundamental social institutions. We now live in a world of great social machines—massive bureaucracies of corporations, governments, trade unions, health systems, universities, even church bureaucracies. But despite the continuing achievements of these institutions, fundamental contradictions mark their stated purpose.

For example, the modern medical system has the marvelous technological capacity to transplant hearts and to remove tumors inside the brain. But it does not seriously challenge the threat of nuclear war, nor the plague of abortion, nor truly care for the poor of the earth. Further, as medicine becomes increasingly technocratic, it becomes ever more isolated from powerful spiritual forms of healing.

Modern trade unions become ever more sophisticated in their use of computers for mobilization of members. But so often union members are turned into passive consumers of union services, rather than the active shapers of a movement of a pride-filled solidarity in work. Similarly, having often grown out of religious roots (for example, the British labor movement partly out of the Methodist Church or the American labor movement partly out of Catholic religious support), the labor movement seems increasingly divorced from the spiritual energies which once nourished it.

Modern churches dramatically expand their professional competence, especially in social action. But the laity express a deep spiritual hunger often not addressed by the professionals. Or the professionals seem to offer a spirituality not rooted in ordinary life. It seems that a covert secularism or privatization of spirituality unconsciously invades even the religious institution.

Modern capitalist corporations often turn workers, including managers, into cogs for the economic machine. Communist state enterprises, allegedly controlled by the working class, in fact echo this process often in harsher form. In both cases, so often human needs and dignity do not seem to count. Labor seems to become a tool for the maximization of corporate profit or state power.

The technocratic ethos deepens, especially as corporate-controlled or state-controlled television replaces family, religion, and school as the primary shaper of values. This happens most visibly in capitalist economic advertising or communist political propaganda, but also in other programming.

Modern governments all over the world, whether capitalist or communist, absorb extraordinary percentages of capital, personnel, and materials for purposes of national security. Some even govern by repression and torture in the name of national security. But humanity and the earth become ever more insecure. Shallow critiques of this hyper-militarization blame the military, but the root causes are deeper.

Modern universities, the proponents and nurturers of the mechanistic understanding of science, seem increasingly converted into servants of the process of uprooted bureaucratization. They appear to teach their students how to integrate themselves with modern culture, despite its destructive direction. These universities pursue a supposedly value free and objective mode of inquiry, resulting, however, in a value-less society.

In sum, if we push the modern mechanistic vision to its extreme, its modern dream of freedom points toward an enslaving fatalism, while the modern promise of progress threatens destruction. The fatalism and destruction are at once ecological, social, and spiritual.

Experience of Work

All these institutions—health centers, trade unions, churches, corporations, governments, universities—function only because of the work of the people in them. Goodness and authentic creativity still mark much of their experience. No doubt many people working in these institutions see the destructiveness which accompanies the good side of their work, and wish it could be altered. But so often they feel powerless—like little pieces of a giant machine. In so many cases, the machine built by their work, or the work of others, now controls them.

Sometimes working people repress these critical and creative feelings and surrender their dignity in work. Workers may fail to develop a commitment to their work by treating their job as something foreign to their real interests, or working only for reasons extrinsic to work itself.

For example, if I have no creative voice in my work, I can make up for it by the purchase of designer clothes or the latest stereo equipment. I may work then not for the meaning of work itself, which is to realize the creativity of the earth, to enrich human community, and to deepen our unity with the Creator. No, I may work only to get money for the things I can buy—as compensation for my alienation. Yet the very compensation deepens the alienation.

Of course, once again this is not the whole story. Many good things also come from modern work. We could wax long and eloquent about the marvels of modern technology, flowing from the creativity of modern science. But we need to look here at the final effect. What is the ultimate gain of marvelous accomplishments if the fundamental life system of the planet is threatened? All gains would be lost in a common destruction.

This is a harsh criticism. Its point is not to reject what is good in modern work, rather to preserve it from destruction.

Cycles of Rest and Creativity

One way that modern culture destroys life is by making people work so much, not only in their jobs, but even when they are consuming. We call this the rat race. It so often seems that there is no time to enjoy life. We are always on the run. Our work and our possessions consume us. As a result there seems too little time in life to help marriages grow, to bring children into the world and to nurture them, to care for the elderly, to build up the local community. Everything becomes work, but a work which often fails to renew life.

Without the cyclical rhythm of creation and recreation, work becomes slavery. God gave us the commandment of the sabbath, that is of rest, because without rest the creative process turns destructive. The earth needs to rest, otherwise its fruit-fulness will be lost. The social community needs to rest and to play, otherwise we grow violent. We all need to rest with God in loving prayer, in order that we not lose contact with the mysterious Source of our creativity.

Rest is thus essential to the purpose of work—ecologically, socially, and spiritually. It keeps nature fruitful, prevents humans from being slaves, and taps into divine creativity. Without rest there is no room for new life. Unless renewed by rest, work brings destruction.

Yet while some work too much, others are not allowed to work at all. We call them the unemployed, but they are humans whose creativity has been denied. Rather than the compulsion of the rat race, these denied workers experience boredom. So the other side of the rat race is the pit of boredom.

Both phenomena are interrelated products of our modern culture's interpretation of work. Modern civilization has divided God's rhythm of work and rest into two groups of humans—those who are pressured to work compulsively as in a rat race, and those who are blocked from work and consigned instead to the pit of unemployment. Why is not the work shared with the unemployed, so that all might rest and all might work?

The structural sin of unemployment is a fundamental assault on human dignity. It denies the image of God the Creator in the unemployed. It refuses to give them a social place to exercise their co-creativity with nature, with other humans, and with God.

Priority of Labor

In his encyclical *Laborem Exercens*, Pope John Paul II calls the social degradation of work by this modern mechanistic civilization the inversion of the priority of labor.[7] By the priority of labor he means that work should be a process consciously and creatively shaped by labor, that is by workers themselves. But modern materialistic ideologies have seen workers mostly as instruments of production.

Our modern ideology of liberalism (or capitalism) makes workers tools of the free market. Workers are seen as commodities (or, in the pope's words, merchandise), whose labor is to be bought like raw materials or energy. When a lot of labor is needed, the free market buys a lot. When a lot is no longer needed, the free market lets it go into unemployment. Then, if there are many extra workers, labor can be bought at a cheap price. All this is considered the scientific law of the free market. It is given the same absolute character in modern times that the divine right of kings had in the Middle Ages.

Marxism rebelled against this domination of labor by capital through the free market. But when Marxism tried to restore the priority of labor (that is the participation and creativity of workers), it largely failed. Why? Because it built up only the priority of the state. Rejecting the free market, it elevated the state as the organizing principle of the work process. But workers were still reduced to mechanistic forces of production. Capital still dominated labor, but now through government rather than through the market.

In addition Marxism, more overtly than capitalism, tried to repress spiritual energies. Capitalism's liberal ideology seductively privatized and so marginalized religion. But Marxism tended to see spiritual consciousness as a political obstacle to progress. It tried formally to repress religion with state power. Later, failing to eliminate religion, it settled for state control.

Erosion of Human Communion

The modern mechanistic vision, guided by either modern ideology, militates against human community. We see the effects every day in the weakening of family, in spread of mass technological abortion, in the decline of family, neighborhoods, and communal life, in the intensifying process of bureaucratization, and in our deepening alienation from nature.[8]

Again I do not mean to say that all modern work has this social effect. So many people in the work process continue to nourish human community, and to resist hiding in a bureaucratized or privatized refuge. But their social creativity often seems to flourish in spite of our mechanistic civilization, not because of it.

Gratefully residual ethnic traditions, drawing on premodern cultural heritages, continue to defend community. But even these traditions erode. As our lives are more and more shaped by large bureaucratic organizations, it seems harder to sustain these traditions.

But not only is the human dimension of work degraded. So too are its ecological and spiritual dimensions.

Erosion of Ecological Communion

The ecological degradation became clear only in recent times. Just as the inversion of the priority of labor is the root of the crisis of the social side of the work process, so the inversion of what we might call the priority of nature is the root of the crisis of its ecological side.

According to the principle of the priority of nature, nature is the source of life, even of human life, and so of human creativity. Humanity is not a category separate from nature, but part of nature's ecology.

Yet rather than understanding nature as the created source of our own creativity and understanding ourselves as a dependent part of nature, we tend to see nature as an extrinsic and inert object available for our limitless exploitation and manipulation. As a result, nature is slowly converted from the created and living source of human creativity to a valueless object of exploitation and destruction.[9] But the destruction of nature is simultaneously the destruction of humanity, for humanity is part of nature's ecology.

We now watch the poisoning of the ground waters, rivers, and streams from industrial and agricultural pollutants. We read reports of the killing of trees and fish by acid rain. In the very food we eat, we worry about the additives and preservatives, even a steady diet of antibiotics in poultry and beef. Recently we became aware of a puncture in the ozone shield at one of the polar caps. All this is the outcome of degraded work.

As Pope John Paul constantly points out in his speeches and writings, life on earth is now threatened with extinction.

We face the risk of ecological suicide through slow contamination of the sub-systems of air, earth, and water, or through rapid holocaust by nuclear war. This fear of destruction comes not from nature itself, but from what modern work does to nature.

Erosion of Spiritual Communion

Finally, ecologically and socially destructive work proves profoundly anti-spiritual. It does this by denying the religious meaning of the earth, treating it instead as a dead object open to plunder. It also does this by denying the divine rhythm of creativity in human labor and treating workers instead as an abstract market commodity or a political instrument.

The attack on ecological and human dignity is ultimately an attack on the Creator, the source of the dignity of both and the one whose presence is analogically imaged in creation.[10] The modern degradation of work implicitly tries to eliminate the image of God in creation.

Yet I believe that the root of this blocking of the divine image does not flow simply from the mechanistic ideologies of modern times. Paradoxically I believe it flows more deeply, though indirectly and certainly not intentionally, from the anti-worldly orientation of the classical and modern spiritualities of western Christianity. But that is a matter for the next chapter.

Summary

In this chapter, I have proposed that we are experiencing a fundamental crisis of the work process. This crisis is rooted in the loss of cyclical renewal, and takes a threefold expression. First, it is undermining the ecological viability of the earth itself. Second, it is eroding the fabric of human community,

beginning with the family, and polarizing life into massive bureaucracies of production and privatized yet disintegrating
ghettos of individualistic consumption. Third, it is eliminating
the spiritual depth of life. This threefold crisis was traced directly to the mechanistic root metaphor which lies at the foundation of the modern cultural consciousness, with the
suggestion of a deeper indirect root in the western spiritual
tradition's flight from the world.

2.
Work as Co-Creation

Although we are seldom told of its spiritual significance, work is intended by God to be one of the most profound ways of experiencing the divine presence in the world. Even when we do not advert to it, work remains in its inner depth a spiritual experience. Along with family, it is a fundamental way by which we humans share in renewing and deepening the creativity of our species and of its wider ecological source in the earth—all in intimate communion with the creativity of the Creator.

In exploring a spirituality of work as co-creation, I will (1) examine some of the dualist and reductionist views of work which prevent us from realizing work's profoundly spiritual meaning, (2) sketch the meaning of human work as ecological, social, and divine co-creation, and (3) suggest some fundamental criteria for distinguishing holy or authentic work from evil or degraded work.

These reflections are intended as an antidote to the modern degradation of work examined in Chapter 1. They are drawn from Pope John Paul II's encyclical *Laborem Exercens*, from creation-centered spirituality, and from the insights of the ecological movement.

Distorted and Reductionist Interpretations of Work

Three common interpretations of work prevent us from realizing its spiritual significance. The first two come to us from western Christian spiritualities, one classical and the other modern. The third comes from modern ideologies. All three are essentially dualist in character, with the net result of offering distorted and reductionist interpretations.

I undertake this critique of classical and modern western Christian spiritualities and of modern western rationalist ideologies because, as mentioned earlier, these spiritualities and ideologies no longer appear able to supply the primary guidance for our civilizations. But I do not mean that these spiritualities and ideologies had no creative role in their prior contexts, nor even that they will no longer play a creative role in the future. My only proposal is that they cannot be the heart of our post-modern interpretation of work.

1. *The Classical Religious/Secular Dualism*

The first misinterpretation comes to us from the hierarchical spiritualities of the classical Christian west, which divided Jesus' disciples into those of the higher way (religious and clergy) and those of the lower way (laity). This distortion causes us to consider as religious only those works done by professional religious elites—clergy or individuals in religious life. A spiritual understanding of work is limited to work done in religious institutions or by specifically clerical or religious people. Other workers, works, and workplaces are called secular, meaning non-religious.

This secular/religious or sacred/profane distinction is actually older than Christianity. It goes back to the origins of human culture, but was taken up by Christianity from Greco-Roman sources.

This dualism referred to people who do these religious

works as having vocations from God, as if other forms of work were not also vocations from God. Praying for vocations meant praying for these religious elite roles, thus falling into the trap of this first distortion of work which forgets its inherently spiritual dimension.

In this dualistic model, secular work was addressed by these professional religious elites through moral directives issued from the religious sector to secular society, but seldom in terms of a spirituality which arises from within the work process. By contrast, Pope John Paul II's encyclical *Laborem Exercens,* offering a profound spirituality of work, is a remarkable new departure.

To find the key to this classical distinction between religious and secular work, it is helpful to look at the root meaning of the word secular. The word comes from the Latin *saeculum,* which was used to describe historical ages, but actually means cycles. The word *saeculum* in turn comes from the Latin word *secus,* which means sex.

This suggests that classical high spiritualities saw history in an essentially sexual manner, meaning that historical ages were subject to the same cycles of birth and death that required sexual reproduction in nature. In contrast to modernity, which tends to see sexuality only as an instrument for private pleasure or personal fulfillment, the classical world viewed sexuality as a requirement of species subject to death. Because the members of a species die, the species must reproduce. Consequently in Greek mythology *eros* (the sexual urge) and *thanatos* (the death urge) were closely linked.

Thus, for the classical religious/secular dichotomy, religious meant that which breaks with the sexual cycles of nature and history to reach for God beyond the created world. The secular or sexual world was seen as imprisoned in sexual cycles of reproduction. This reaching for God beyond the reproductive cycles of birth and death is called a spirituality of transcendence, meaning rising above the cycles of secular life.

Because of their transcendent style, classical western spiritualities tended to require of those who would seriously pursue holiness that they reject the biological and historical cycles of material concerns. In Catholicism the requirement of celibacy for Latin rite clergy and members of religious orders comes partly from this attempt to transcend secular life. Celibacy, of course, remains an evangelical charism, but its original evangelical form was never a way of separating out religious elites. Rather it was an unstructured charism found within the community of Jesus' disciples, and in Jesus himself who presented himself as a lay teacher of the Pharisaic school of Judaism. Yet the concept of a separate religious life, apart from the main community of Jesus' disciples (the laity), became the cultural foundation of the classical model of spirituality. This transcendently religious model, uprooted from biology and history, began in Christianity with monasticism, and was later extended to the Latin rite secular clergy.

The error of this perspective was not transcendence itself (a profound and permanent dimension of our spiritual tradition), nor the charism of celibacy (again a cherished gift always found throughout the Christian community). The error was more subtle and twofold—first to forget that transcendence alone does not fully disclose God's revelation, and second to convert the charism of celibacy into a state of life requirement for professional religious elites.

Such a one-sided focus on transcendence fails to celebrate the Creator's intimate and fertile presence within creation's dynamic processes. The path which remembers this alternate dimension of revelation is a spirituality of immanence.

Classical spirituality first put immanence on a lower plane than the higher way of transcendence. Then, failing to cultivate its mystery, it began to lose contact with God's immanent presence through creation. This was expressed in Latin by classical spiritual writers as the desired *fuga mundi*, that is flight from the world.

By contrast a spirituality of immanence meets God not by rejecting creation, but by embracing it— by celebrating God's manifestation through creation, and by seeking the healing of creation's woundedness from sin.

Similarly a spirituality of immanence does not reject sexuality as a block to the holy, but celebrates the profound religious mystery disclosed in sexuality itself, while seeking to heal any sinful wounding of the sexual disclosure of mystery.

Finally a spirituality of immanence does not reject secular work with its material cares, but celebrates those cares as a way of linking with the Creator's own cares.

Hence, from the viewpoint of a spirituality of immanence, the secular or sexual world is God's primary revelation. Therefore secular work, like secular sexuality and indeed all of secular creation, is profoundly religious.

The immanent spiritual metaphor of sexuality is in turn a key to the spiritual meaning of work. It teaches us that work is a broadening of that co-creative fertility begun in sexuality. If authentic, it deepens the life process as the holy expression of communitarian creativity and hence is worshipful work. If degraded, it blocks the life process, becomes the fragmenting expression of destruction, and hence is idolatrous work.

A variant of the classical religious/secular dichotomy sees work as a distraction from prayer. In this view work is necessary because of our bodily or earthly nature. We have to do it, but it would be better if we didn't. Then we could be busy with heavenly things. But (for this distortion) accepting our unfortunate earthiness, we can make of work an instrument which leads to prayer. The religious meaning of such work, in this view, comes not from the meaning of the work itself, but from our psychological disposition toward it.

Work is also often seen as a way of keeping us from idle distractions, which might tempt us away from God. Work assumes a protective function, but for something outside itself. Here prayer really begins only when work ends. Work is a "lower" good, the servant of the "higher" good of prayer. The framework is again hierarchical.

As a result of this classical distortion work gains status to the degree that it seems to be removed from the earth with its sexual cycles. Thus jobs which get our hands dirty or require physical labor, especially jobs which deal with waste products or directly with the earth itself, are seen as inferior to jobs which keep our hands clean and require only mental labor. Mental labor becomes more heavenly, while manual labor remains earthly.

Our educational system reinforces this dichotomy. For example, in high school, college-bound students may study the theory of the internal combustion engine used in automobiles, but only non-college bound students taking a shop course actually put their hands on greasy car motors during school hours.

A more intense version of this distortion is to see work as a curse for original sin. This assumes that if there had been no sin, there would be no work, or that work is so corrupted by sin that it has no creative religious root without redemption. In the latter case, grace externally triumphs over corrupt nature, rather than healing nature from within by deepening and correcting its still vital, if wounded, creativity.

This pessimistic view of work is a stronger tendency in the Reformation strand of Christianity, whereas the mainstream of the classical Catholic tradition tended to see work more positively but hierarchically—simply as "lower" than the "higher" "religious" way of unworldly transcendent contemplation.

The classical dualism of religious/secular, understood as higher/lower ways, gets transposed in the modern cultural context to entirely different terms. But the modern terms still maintain the dualism with an equally reductionist interpretation of both poles.

2. *The Modern Public/Private Dualism*

Modern spiritualities have tended to revise the classical dualism by separating the objective/subjective dimensions of experience into separate technological and psychological regions. The classical higher/lower split of transcendence versus immanence shifts into the modern psyche/techne split of interiority versus exteriority. These modern spiritualities of interiority tended to alienate work to a public, objective, secular technological world, and to confine spirituality to a private, subjective, psychological world detached from society.

The modern cultural meaning of technological work is thus cut off not only from formal spiritualities, but also from the psychological dimension of subjectivity. As a result labor is seen mechanistically as a market, a force, or a factor of production to be exploited, organized, or managed, but not as a spiritual and subjective co-creator. Simultaneously spirituality is isolated from the objective social structures of our macro-experience (the fruit of human work) and collapsed into the individualized and privatized subjectivity of psychological interiority.

Again classical spiritualities sought escape from the immanently sacred meaning of work by trying to rise above the sexual cycles of time and space into contemplative transcendence. By contrast modern spiritualities tried to escape the exteriorly sacred meaning of work by retreating into the interior realm. Thus the modern spiritual way is centered on psychological interiority, in contrast to the classical way of philosophical transcendence. Institutionally it is expressed as the shift in dominance from the monastery to the retreat house, from contemplation to spiritual direction.

The modern spiritual life becomes then a matter of internal psychological processes, guided by a kind of religious psychologist. Appropriately the best location for this process is a retreat, traditionally a place where one was removed from social community and from public life.

Typically the spiritual director had training in psychological science, and helped the retreatant to discern the presence of God in interior psychological events. But the director was not expected to have any training in social science, nor was the retreatant expected to focus on events in the objective, public world nor on its work process.

As with transcendence, the error here was not interiority itself, nor even spiritual direction, and certainly not retreats, all of which enrich our spiritual understanding of the self. (Indeed we need to integrate the classical sense of transcendence and the modern sense of interiority with what I call post-modern spirituality.) Rather the error was the privatization and individuation of interiority in isolation from the external and public processes of nature and history, as well as the implicit denial of the subjective and spiritual dimensions of work.

Such individualistic retreats, though a great resource in their place, are nonetheless not the main path to a post-modern Christian spirituality. For one thing, in their present style they are not financially feasible for the majority of the laity, in whom a post-modern spirituality must be centered. Nor are they suited to the intensely familial and communal life of most laity. (In the past seldom did retreat houses have double beds for spouses or bunk beds for children.) In their model, to be with God one left family and work.

A communal spirituality of creativity is sorely needed by modern society. As modern religious elites are tempted to retreat deeper into psychological interiority, and in turn take many of the laity with them, or else fail to teach the laity an adequate lay spirituality, the secular world is stripped of public spiritual meaning.

We have reviewed how the transcending philosophical contemplation of hierarchical classical spiritualities and the retreating psychological journey of privatizing western spiritualities indirectly and unintentionally assisted the public triumph of destructive modern ideologies. But let us look now at the dualisms of modern secular ideologies.

3. *Work as an Instrument of "The Economy"*

In this third distortion, flowing from modern ideologies, work receives great attention and absorbs much of our energy. But this is only for what is objectified as "the economy" with its process of production and consumption, all seen as outside of subjective and religious experience. With each of the modern ideological types, while the basic framework is the same, the emphasis is different.

In the capitalist sphere, the ideological tendency is to instrumentalize work for "the economy" through the market. Work serves the economy by expanding the market, and in turn by expanding consumption. Indeed, in the capitalist ideology, labor itself is viewed mainly as a market, as revealed in the term labor market.

In the communist sphere, the tendency is to instrumentalize work for "the economy" through the state. Usually this means that the purpose of the work process is to maximize state power, or the scientific control of the party, with the promise (if not the achievement) of high consumption. Here labor is not viewed as a market to be exploited by economic elites, but rather as a force (as in labor force) to be organized by political elites.

Social democratic or democratic socialist ideologies are simply a mix of these two positions, and move on the same instrumental modern terrain.

In both cases labor is an object of production (and alternately of consumption), with only the elites, be they economic or political, granted a subjective or creative role. Labor becomes then a market or a force used by elites for purposes external to labor itself, with creativity ascribed to "the economy" and to the elites who preside over it.

For both modern ideologies, capitalist or communist or whatever in between, the process of economic production is understood in a way which flattens nature's regenerative cycles and society's regenerative cycles, thereby repressing the reproductive side of work. This is most clear in the ecological process, where modern work undermines society's ability to sustain itself as part of nature. But it also happens within the social dimension of work, as our modern economic models undermine family and neighborhood, and so weaken the ability of the community to renew itself across time and space. For example, the graying of the mass industrial societies of the west is a much commented phenomenon with serious negative economic consequences.

Especially important here is the shifting female role in late modern culture. The struggle to overcome patriarchy is a creative contribution of modern feminism. Unfortunately that is not all there is to say.

In the name of liberal modernization, the cultural role of woman is increasingly adapted to the culturally normative male role, itself long since alienated from the cycles of reproduction. Just as at the macro level modern work produces the nuclear arms race, threatening to destroy the reproductive capacity of the whole planet, so at the micro level modern sexual freedom produces the triumph of abortion, threatening life at the level of the womb. One form of killing is outward, the other inward. One is actively aggressive, the other passively aggressive. But the mutually destructive consequences are negatively reinforcing.

Thus the modern understanding of woman, although correct in its condemnation of patriarchy, becomes assimilation to a biologically uprooted male model, further compounding the modern cultural crisis. We might say that the heart of the modern crisis is not simply the techne-psyche split of objectivity from subjectivity, but more profoundly the productive-reproductive split of mechanistically linear production crushing the rhythmic cycles of ecological and social reproduction.

Both modern ideologies have taken seriously the hidden lesson implicitly taught by classical and modern spiritualities. The hidden lesson is that worldly technological work of itself lacks deep spiritual or subjective meaning. As a result, in the western cultural tradition, human work was first spiritually forgotten and then ideologically instrumentalized.

Thus, despite the great gulf between modern spiritualistic and ideological interpretations of life, they both share this common failure to value work as a subjective and religious experience. Either they psychologically retreat from it or they technologically instrumentalize it, and in both cases for some separate purpose. We might say that modern spiritualities and modern ideologies became two sides of the same coin of modern culture, each feeding the other, each carrying in its original context its own contribution, but both now immersed in a common and deep cultural crisis.

If we return to the metaphor of sexuality, the similarity between classical and modern western spiritualities and modern western ideologies is apparent at yet a deeper level. Both seek to break with the sexual-cyclical nature of creation. The classical and modern spiritualities sought to escape the sexual world with its cycles by stressing first transcendence over immanence, then subjectivity over objectivity. For Catholic religious elites this means breaking with the process of reproduction. Modern ideologies make a similar break by stressing production over reproduction, in turn undermining the ecological, social and spiritual reproduction of life.

Could it be then that there is some unintended and in-direct, yet real connection between Western culture's classical demand for a religious celibate professional elite witnessing to a non-regenerative interpretation of the holy, and the subse-quent anti-reproductive drive of modern western ideologies as revealed by their extraordinary commitment to birth control and abortion, the social erosion of family and community, the ecological undermining of the planetary life system, and the loss of public spiritual depth?

This is a hard question for religious elites, but perhaps we need to raise harsh questions on the religious side, just as the religious side has been willing to raise hard questions of technological structures.

Finally, the modern work process with its stress on pro-duction over reproduction undermines the spiritual dimension of work. In many modern work situations, many people no longer seem to experience creativity, but rather a crass in-strumentalization, a spiritual flattening, and isolation from na-ture. The outcome is often pseudo-compensation through alienated consumption in the rat race, or still worse exile from work through unemployment.

While the greatest structural sin is unemployment, the more common personal sin for those of us who are employed is to cooperate in the instrumentalization of our work, by view-ing it mainly as a means to consumption. In this case work becomes simply the place where we earn money to buy con-sumer goods. Such consumer goods may be frivolous or nec-essary, but the focus is on the act of consumption, not on the cyclical holism of production and reproduction linked in turn to the subjective/objective creativity of labor and the spiritual depth of its secularity.

This modern ideological interpretation of work is not so much a rejection as a reduction of the meaning of work. Certainly much work is an important means of earning a living. The error is not to assert this, but to stop there. For work is also something much more.

While this reduction comes to us from secular sources, again may it not be the indirect fruit of the long devaluing of secular work within the west's dominant spiritual traditions? If tendencies in our spiritual traditions identified only certain works as religious, viewed other work as a distraction from spirituality, or saw work as a curse for sin or totally corrupted by it, then should it be any wonder that our modern social world (a product of work), at the very moment of dramatic technological breakthrough, simultaneously experiences a loss of spiritual meaning? Similarly should it be any wonder that our society seems to forget the inner meaning of work and to focus instead on consumerism?

To heal the destructive effects both from the forgetfulness of the spiritual meaning of work by classical and modern spiritualities, and from the public degrading of work by modern ideologies, we need to recover the spiritual depth of work itself.

The Spiritual Meaning of Work as Co-Creation

Perhaps too much time has been spent already on interpretations of work which block our discovery of its spiritual meaning. It might have been better to unfold this spiritual meaning directly, indirectly causing the distortions to fade. But I found that it was necessary first to wrestle with these distortions within myself, in order to be free to celebrate the truth of work. Perhaps that is not the way for everyone, but it has been my way. In any case, let us turn now to the postmodern vision of work as co-creation.

As creation-centered spiritual writers like Teilhard de Chardin, Gibson Winter, Matthew Fox, Charlene Spretnak, Brian Swimme, and Thomas Berry have reminded us, the starting point for spirituality is the affirmation of creation.[11] Creation is the fundamental doctrine of theology. Without creation there is no voice to offer blessings, no creature to sin or be redeemed, no one to theologize, and nothing to theologize about. It is in the context of continuing creation as foundational that we first need to understand the spiritual meaning of human work.

For Catholic theology, creation was not totally corrupted by sin, but retains a foundational goodness. Thus for classical Catholic theology, a foundation principle was that grace builds on nature. This was a classical transcendent and consequently hierarchical statement of the insight, signaling that nature was below, while grace was extrinsically above. Together they functioned like a two-story building.

From the perspective of a spirituality of immanence, however, we might say that grace works through nature. Thus grace becomes not something descending extrinsically upon creation below, but rather something revealed from within the inner depths of creation—coming from the very source of creation, deeper than creation itself, healing creation's woundedness, and intensifying its co-creativity with the Creator. Our work thus, if it both unfolds and heals creation, partakes of both God's natural and supernatural (a transcendent term) revelation.

In such a perspective, sin becomes that perversion which tries to block the creativity of creation. Sin is anti-creation. Sin and grace can be thus counterposed as anti-creation versus a healing-intensifying re-creation.

In exploring the relationship of this affirmation of creation to a spirituality of work, I would like to make three points.

1. *The Developmental Process of Creation*

Thanks to the micro-electronic revolution with its computerized electronic telescopes and electronic microscopes, we are now experiencing the birth of a post-modern physics. This post-modern physics tells us that creation is not something over and done with, or simply maintained by cyclical renewal of the same patterns. Rather we are discovering that creation is a developmental process, a continuing journey, an unfolding flower. Cycles are basic to it, but within the cyclical rhythm there is developmental creativity which brings ever more powerful consciousness by life of its communal creativity—ecological, social, and divine.

This process begins its creativity with the primal explosion of matter, spreads outward in the formation of the galaxies (still unfinished), and deepens still more with the developmental emergence of life—from the simplest forms up to the mammals. Finally it achieves reflective consciousness in the human species. In human beings (and perhaps other rational creatures in other solar systems?) the universe begins to think.

Human consciousness is not simply the private property of human beings who are systemically distinct from and superior to the rest of planet earth or to the rest of the universe. No, human consciousness, as Pierre Teilhard de Chardin so mystically expressed, is the evolutionary point at which planet earth, and perhaps the whole universe, begins its conscious phase.[12]

Hence the revelation of immanent creativity, and its struggle between sin and grace, needs to be understood as an unfolding journey or a deepening story. As creation continues to unfold around us, so too God's natural revelation itself continues to unfold. Our work is in turn a part of that unfolding process of creation, and part of God's natural revelation.

2. *Development of Consciousness and Culture*

Human consciousness, a dramatic stage in the unfolding revelation of creation, is itself a developmental process. The transforming process of human consciousness across time and space is what we call human culture. Culture itself is unfolding, constantly reshaping the world in myriad ways, each reflecting the developmental creativity of the human imagination.

Thomas Berry suggests that the developmental journey of human consciousness has created three distinct stages of culture, and is presently creating a fourth.[13] In describing these stages, I will use my own terms, basically chronological, and describe them in my own way.

1. *The Primal Stage:* This stage is based on speech (oral tradition) and refers to the tribal-shamanistic phase of human culture. It celebrates God's spiritual revelation in nature (animism). Spiritually this is the stage of immanence, symbolized by the earth mother as a symbol of the cosmos which dwells within the maternal womb.

2. *The Classical Stage:* This stage is based on handwriting and refers to the priestly-hierarchical civilizations out of which the world religions of a holy book were born. Its spirituality is one of transcendence symbolized by the image of the sky father presiding over the cosmos as extrinsic creation.

3. *The Modern Stage:* This stage is based on mass printing, and refers to the industrial-pietistic society, producing the dichotomy of non-religious or even anti-religious public ideologies and privatized spiritualities. It is the spirituality of interiority symbolized by the sibling rivalry between a passively aggressive feminine psychological interiority (including religion and literature, as well as therapy) and an actively aggressive masculine technological exteriority of the industrial world.

4. *The Post-Modern Stage:* This stage is based on electronics and refers to an ecological-mystical society leading to an ecological reformulation of humanity's religious traditions.

Its spirituality is one of co-creativity, symbolized by the fertile sexual embrace of the feminine and masculine symbols.

These four stages constitute the on-going journey of human culture, and each stage bears a different view of work and of spirituality. The primal stage mystically understood the immanent presence of the Mystery in all creation, but this understanding was limited to a cyclical framework lacking techno-scientific consciousness. The classical stage unfolded human technological consciousness beyond the limits of nature's cycles, but also uprooted spirituality from everyday life, including work, into a dualistic transcendence. The modern stage developed enormously humanity's interior subjective depth and exterior technological power, but also began to split the world into separate private and public realms, with a privatization of spirituality and a public degrading of work, in turn undermining the reproductive foundations of work's productivity.

As I have developed elsewhere, each dominant stage of human spirituality is grounded on the means of communication of its cultural context.[14] Thus the dominance of a nature-oriented spirituality of immanence corresponded to the communal primal stage of human culture where the only means of communications was speech. The world-fleeing spirituality of transcendence corresponded to the hierarchical classical stage of human culture where handwriting created a new religious elite separated from the popular community. The individualistic spirituality of interiority corresponded to the modern stage of human culture where printing created a fragmenting and privatizing social experience. The fresh dynamic-holistic spirituality of creativity corresponds to the post-modern stage of human culture where electronic communications link all information and make possible a more innovative society.

Each of these stages has in turn its dominant referent in the sexually rooted religious imagination. For immanence it is the earth mother. For transcendence it is the sky father. For interiority it is the sibling rivalry between a psychologized womb and a technologized phallus. For creativity it is the fertile sexual union.

Immanence, transcendence, interiority, and creativity are the four successive stages of dominant spiritualities in the western journey. The present challenge is not to eliminate any, but to integrate the received two into the new framework of co-creativity.

But although immanence, interiority, and transcendence need to remain a profound dimension of Christian spirituality, they will not any longer be the defining center of Christian spirituality. For they do not provide an adequate spiritual ground to rescue the late modern world of Western culture from its extinguishing of life.

STAGES OF HUMAN SPIRITUALITY

CULTURAL CONTEXT	COMMUNICATIONS MEDIA	SPIRITUALITY	SEXUAL SYMBOL
Primal	Speech	Immanence	Earth Mother
Classical	Writing	Transcendence	Sky Father
Modern	Printing	Interiority	Sibling Rivalry
Post-Modern	Electronics	Creativity	Fertile Union

For an evangelical healing of the crisis of modern culture, we need rather a spirituality which discovers the deep and holy meaning of work in its communal relationships with nature and society, including the objective social structures which it produces, and ultimately with the Creator. This means a spirituality which recovers the secular experience of God's creative immanence and public exteriority.

It thus becomes the task of the post-modern stage of human culture to link spirituality with this techno-scientific consciousness, to link science and technology with human subjectivity, and to link all with the cyclical rhythm of the ecological-human-divine creativity of work.

In this post-modern framework, we are called to become explicitly conscious of the spiritual meaning of work. This means that we need to rediscover work as the way we humans, one particular expression of nature, become artistic co-creators with the rest of nature, with the whole human community, and with the divine Creator. We are the point (on planet earth) at which God's creative drive through nature is revealed in created consciousness. If our work is good work, in it we discover ourselves as the artistic co-creators of the species and of the earth, in turn all flowing from divine creativity. Thus we encounter the Creator in and through the creativity of our work within nature and history.

The experience of this world as unfolding co-creation becomes the most profound natural basis for our meeting the Mystery. A privileged place for experiencing this world as unfolding creation is our own work of sustaining and transforming the world. The Creator is present in every point and at every moment of the universe's creative drive, including human work. Work thus becomes our share in the loving expression of the Creator's artistic creativity.

3. All Work Is Religious

It should now be clear that all work is profoundly religious, even if we are not conscious of that fact. Work is nothing less than human participation in the divine creativity expressed in the creativity of the universe. Work is a fundamental cultural way by which we reveal God's actively creative love. Work is a fundamental cultural place where we express our dynamic rootedness in the rest of our natural world, and ultimately in the Creator.

How imbalanced then to suggest today that only certain works are religious. Or that work is a distraction from knowing God. Or that work is a curse from sin. Or that work is only a means for buying things. Such theological and ideological distortions of work ultimately deny the religious significance of creation and blind us to the Creator's revelation.

Work then is a fundamentally religious act. It is a basic source of dynamic unity with the Creator. What we call in a narrow sense "religious" is only legitimately religious to the degree that it affirms, heals, and celebrates the basic religious experience of life. Work is thus a foundation of worship, and worship is authentic only when it grows out of work.

Holy Work and Evil Work

The creativity of work may be blocked by structures which disfigure its meaning. Thus work may be reduced to oppression by slave labor, or to drudgery by denial of human creativity, or work may be denied entirely to people through unemployment. In addition, work may be free, apparently creative, yet devoted to destructive purposes, like poisoning the earth, brutalizing people, or blaspheming the Creator. So it becomes necessary to distinguish between authentic work and degraded work. I will describe authentic work as holy and degraded work as evil.

Holy work opens the work process to the creativity of the human species, of the rest of the universe, and ultimately of the Creator. By contrast evil work blocks all three interrelated sources of creativity. When this threefold creativity of work (human, ecological, and divine) is blocked, work grows destructive.

The distinguishing of holy work from evil work occurs socially at the personal and institutional levels. At the personal level, each of us wrestles with our own individual vocation, namely how we will apply the energies of our work to sustain and expand this creativity. Similarly at the institutional level, large bodies like trade unions, corporations, and governments struggle over how work will be socially expressed.

At both these levels, we face the danger of allowing work to become evil. But we also have the possibility of allowing our personal work and the work of society to open itself ever more to the creative power of the human community, of the universe, and, at the deepest level, of the Divine Mystery.

These two dimensions—the personal and institutional—are not just set side by side. Rather they are interdependent. On the one hand institutional work emerges from so many personal works. On the other hand personal works are limited or challenged by the opportunities presented by the society's institutions.

Evil work may not be the fault of the actual workers who perform the work. It may not be a particular worker's fault if the work situation fragments human community, stifles human creativity, injures the natural ecology, and shuts out the image of the mystery. Workers may be the victims of evil work, rather than the causes. The work may be imposed on them by a larger institution, as slavery was imposed against the will of the enslaved.

Nonetheless, in the name of the religious vision of authentic work, workers have a religious obligation to struggle against such degrading structures of work and to transform them. Of course how and to what degree such struggle is feasible is a question of prudent judgment.

Yet much of our work seems neither purely holy nor purely evil, but rather seems to fall in the middle ground of ambiguity. Nonetheless, even with ambiguous work the call to holiness is a call to purify work of its ambiguity, to resist its partial degradation, and to make it more clearly holy.

Based on what has been stated thus far, I propose three fundamental ethical criteria for human work to be holy: the ecological, the human, and the divine. These criteria flow from the three creative communions of life which constitute authentically holistic work—again the ecological, the human, and the divine.

These three creative communions of life form a single holistic experience. They are not competitively separated from each other (as in the modern liberal view), nor stacked hierarchically upon each other (as in the classical transcendent view). For example, the human is part of the ecological, that is, humanity lives only within nature, not over against it nor above it. Further co-creation with the divine occurs only in and through the social-ecological communion, which in turn reveals the mystery as its deepest meaning.

1. Communion with Ecological Creativity

Just as contemporary work tends to treat workers as objects to be exploited or managed, so too it often treats the earth as an object to be plundered. As we now know, the end result is an ecological crisis. Work becomes evil when it treats the earth as something to be manipulated and used with no respect for its regenerative cycles or its religious meaning.[15]

As mentioned earlier, the "high" transcendent spiritualities of the classical period, which sought the holy outside this world, may have been a seed for this abuse of the earth. Only after the world was stripped of religious meaning could it be technologically plundered. Further the modern revolution, which linked religious meaning almost exclusively with subjectivity, deepened society's capacity for objective manipulation of the earth, without spiritual celebration of its regenerative function.

By contrast, holy work respects nature by cooperating with it as a partner in the creative process. Holy work learns from nature, is careful never to abuse nature, is conscious of itself as part of nature, and treats nature as sacred. Holy work is ecological work.

Again, one dramatic way that modern work seems to violate nature is, as mentioned earlier, by losing a sense of re-generative cycles. All of nature's life (and we are part of nature) follows a cyclical rhythm of renewal. Yet modern work is pre-dominantly structured on a linear model of driving efficiency. In capitalism this efficiency is measured by profit, and in com-munism by power. All other values are subordinated to this linear technological drive for profit or power. It is this sense of drive without rhythm, of work without rest and play, which makes modern life seem like a rat race. Frantic work may be-come efficient, but destructive. Failing to give life, it begins to take it.

Again, another way the cyclical dimension of renewal needs to be honored bears on waste. Frequently tasks associated with waste (e.g. trash or sewage removal) are held in low es-teem. Yet these are holy tasks in which a special dimension of God is revealed, namely the dimension of the circle by which life appears to die, yet provides the seed for its renewal. The apparent waste of life is a sacred moment of life itself. It is but the hidden moment of life, which reveals the hidden face of God. Waste is the natural cross of the universe, leading to the natural resurrection of life. How important that all work self-consciously take into account its waste products, and at-tempt to recycle them creatively.

2. Communion with Human Creativity

Since reflective consciousness distinguishes human work from the pre-conscious sectors of creation, human work needs to be judged by the criterion of conscious participation in the creative process.

To the degree that workers are treated only as objects to be externally managed into efficient units, or organized into mass blocs, or exploited as an inert resource, without conscious participation in creatively shaping their work, then their dignity and their work is disfigured. Their work becomes evil, though the evil is not necessarily their personal evil. It is rather the evil of the structures and the elites of these structures which treat them as unconscious and uncreative instruments.

By contrast, to the degree that workers are drawn into creatively conscious participation, the work process becomes holy.

Contemporary institutional structures repress participation by becoming bureaucratic and centralized. Participation becomes feasible only to the degree that the institutions of work reorganize themselves into networks of decentralized smaller scale units.[16]

3. *Communion with Divine Creativity*

The final criterion for holy work is that it be self-consciously spiritual. To the degree that this does not happen, we block work's religious depth and its creative energy. As I proposed earlier, if the economy has become anti-spiritual and morally autonomous, from a profound cultural viewpoint the root cause may be less greedy capitalists or power-hungry communists than spiritual elites who tended to become blind to the mystical depth of secular work. If spiritual elites failed to celebrate the religious mystery of work, can we entirely blame the ideologies of the modern world for following through on that failure?

When modern industrial zoning split work and home, where did the religious institutions permit themselves? The churches were built almost exclusively on the home side. It was not that way in the Middle Ages with its guild and manorial chapels.

Even more recently, how often have we heard in sermons that the Sunday liturgy is the cyclical celebration of the religious depth of our work during the week? Contemporary western Christianity often functions almost exclusively on the consumer side of life, relating to the personal life of home, parish, and residential community, but little to the work experience of its believers. Responsible church ministers might consider it important to visit the homes of members of their church community, but how many would think to visit their workplaces?

These three criteria then—communion with ecological, human, and divine creativity—are the norms by which we distinguish holy work from evil work, or authentic work from degraded work. When they are present, the divinely-inspired creativity of the universe continues its unfolding journey. When they are blocked, to some degree the unfolding journey of the universe is blocked. The religious and secular distortions of work are one source of this block. The healing transformation of these blocks requires an ecological-mystical sense of co-creativity which embraces the ecological, human, and divine dimensions of work.

Summary

This chapter has offered a critique of the spiritual and instrumental demeaning of human work by classical and modern western spiritualities and by modern western ideologies. As an alternative it has sketched a post-modern vision of work grounded in an artistic root metaphor seen as arising from post-modern science and post-modern spirituality, both stressing ecological-human-spiritual co-creativity. Finally, it has suggested that the most basic criteria for the moral evaluation of work are the conscious participation in ecological, human, and divine co-creativity. From this viewpoint, a post-modern spirituality of work is not centered in immanence, transcendence, or interiority, important as they remain, but in co-creativity.

In the next chapter, we can explore what such a post-modern spirituality of work might mean for restructuring the modern economy into a post-modern form.

3.
Toward a Holistic Economy

In the first chapter we saw how the modern world is degrading human work. This happens at the very time that work becomes more technologically productive. The combination of technological power with degraded work fundamentally threatens the holistic (ecological, social, and spiritual) communion of life. This danger is being revealed at every level of the life system, from the micro-threat to life in the womb to the macro-threat to the life of the planet.

In the second chapter we saw how the degradation of work flows from three successive reductionisms in the development of western culture, namely the hierarchical dualism of classical spirituality, the privatizing dualism of modern spirituality, and the instrumentalizing dualism of modern ideologies.

But to heal this degradation I proposed that a post-modern culture see human work as profoundly spiritual. This would mean recognizing work as humanity's co-creation with the Creator of the emergent process of planet earth, in turn a part of the emergent process of the whole universe. Authentic work would thus be grounded in celebration of this co-creative communion with the Creator, in turn mediated by communing creativity across our ecological roots and social fabric. In sum, authentic work would express itself as the deepening creativity of ecological, social, and spiritual communion.

For this reason, post-modern culture is called upon not only to intensify the scientific-technological journey, but also to guide it on a course which allows human work to reveal itself in a threefold holism: (1) ecologically as the earth's development process coming to consciousness in the human species, (2) humanly as the social community unfolding the artistry of its communal interaction, in turn deepening of the earth's own communal artistry, and (3) spiritually as the social-ecological whole revealing the divine source of its communal creativity. The pursuit of this task we might describe as the attempt to give birth to a holistic or holy economy.

In exploring the nature and possibility of a holy post-modern economy, we need to set our exploration within the historical journey of human work since the emergence of the human species. Thus we may see the search as part of an ancient, continuing, and unfinished story.

In telling the story, we can summarize the journey by abstracting out of its complex fabric three broad stages unfolded so far, with the threshold of a fourth stage only now revealing itself. Again renaming Thomas Berry's stages, these may be described as (1) the primal, (2) the classical, (3) the modern, and (4) the post-modern. Since the political economy is the objective ground of culture's meaning, and since work is the heart of the political economy, these stages of human culture are more fundamentally stages of human work.

Since we have already probed the modern and classical stages of human culture and their attitude toward work (and sexuality) in Chapters 1 and 2, we may now explore the earliest primal stage and the emerging post-modern stage. Thus we will tap our deepest memories and our richest imagination. It will be, I propose, this recovery of our primal roots along with the exploration of the post-modern imagination which will heal the destructive western legacy of classicism and modernity.

Between this primal memory and post-modern imagination, as we search for a holy economy, we may also ask what the stories of Genesis and Jesus' teaching say to us about the orientation of the Christian community in the healing of modern destructiveness.

Primal Memory: The Holistic Circle of Genesis

The deepest traditions of the human experience, and consequently of the meaning of work, are carried by the tribal cultures of the earth. Through these tribes we come into partial contact with the most ancient ecological, social, and spiritual memories of the human experience.

Yet even these memories have been reshaped by the post-primal stages of human culture. We also tend to read these memories through the lenses of the classical or modern imagination. And often the stories themselves have been rewritten from a modern or classical perspective. So to reach back toward the truly primal, we need to go beyond humanity's historical memory into the realm of the mythic imagination, and there try to enter into the primal consciousness.

Christians can take the Genesis narratives, drawn from the mythic stories told by the Hebrew tribes, as a privileged point of access to the primal myths. Let us see now how this is symbolized in the two creation narratives of Genesis.

1. The First Creation Narrative

According to the first creation story, the so-called "priestly narrative" (Genesis 1:1–31), the creation of humanity is set ecologically within the creation of the universe. Humanity is seen as a high point of creation, but it is not a climax separate from the rest. Every step or day of creation is the creation of something good, in turn revealing richer forms of life. The real crown of creation is not humanity, but the sabbath. Hence creation is not human-centered, but God-centered through the praise of the sabbath.

For this first narrative the human story is clearly part of the wider ecological story. Humanity is special, signaled by reference to the image of God, but not separate. Each day of creation ends with God's seeing that it was good. Finally, perhaps to remind us of the wholeness as well as the goodness of all creation, the narration of the sixth day (when humanity was created) ends not with a statement that humanity is good, but with a statement that everything is good. "God looked at everything he had made, and he found it very good" (verse 31).

The specific human role within the ecology of creation is usually translated as the call to have dominion over the earth and to rule over all the living things. But the image of humanity's relationship to the earth is God's own relationship to creation. And, as we will see in the second creation narrative, the earth is a garden to be cared for. Still later, Jesus will teach us that authority in the community of his disciples (a community which retrieves and deepens the innocence of the garden) is not to be exercised in the manner of "lording over" but as humble service.

So I will take the liberty of translating dominion and rule as care and service, for that is what the tradition teaches us about the meaning of such authority. Following the industrial revolution, dominion and rule have come to mean extrinsic and repressive domination, something not at all in the Genesis narrative.[17]

In addition to seeing work as humanity's process of care and service for the earth from within the ecological process, this first narrative makes several other points which bear on work, in both its productive and its reproductive dimensions.

First, contrary to classical spirituality which tended to

flee the world as a temptation, and contrary to modern spirituality which sought internal subjective refuge from the external objective world, this mythic narrative boldly and repeatedly proclaims the goodness of creation and the inextricable role of humanity within it. To reject the world, either philosophically or psychologically, would be to spurn the goodness of God's creation and humanity's vocation within it.

Second, production is intimately linked with reproduction. The command of care and service for the earth comes in the very same sentence with the command to be fertile and fill the earth. Thus sexuality and work are not separate, but intimately related.

By the way, this should also make it clear that sexuality is not a curse for sin nor the source of sin, but rather at the heart of the human vocation from God. Like all of work, sexuality becomes wounded by sin, but its healing requires recovery of sexuality's primal spiritual depths, something both the classical and modern spiritual traditions tragically failed to cultivate.

Third, the equality and complementarity of male and female are basic to human creation. Patriarchy as the rule of man over woman, with the male representing God and the female representing the earth, is simply not present in this first narrative. Thus the narrative tells us that both male and female, or better both together, reflect the image of God. It tells us that God created humanity in God's own image—male and female God created them (Chapter 1, verse 27). Both sexes are needed to reveal the full image of God and to undertake the vocation to care for the earth and to be sexually fertile.

How different this is from classical Greek thought, carried in turn by so many classical western theologians and spiritual writers, which saw the female as a deformed male incapable of reflecting the divine image. How different too from the classical model which saw the male imaging the divine by turning away from the vocation to cherish the earth and to bring forth children.

2. *The Second Creation Narrative*

The second narrative of creation (Genesis 2:4b–25), often called the "Yahwist narrative," is the story of the garden of Eden. This story, and its subsequent development in the story of sin and the expulsion from the garden (Genesis 3:1–24), is often taken as the basis of justifying patriarchy and a negative view of work and sexuality. But let us look at the narrative through the eyes of the primal imagination.

First, the whole image suggests a holistic view of life's ecological-human-divine community rooted in the intimacy of all three. Humanity is one with its ecology, for the environment is a garden, where humanity and the rest of creation live in a mutual and fruitful intimacy. Humanity is also one with itself socially, for the man and woman are naked but not ashamed. Finally, humanity is one with the Creator, for God is with them in the garden.

Also, the narrative in its original meaning appears not to be a justification of woman's subordination or of sexuality as unholy. But to understand why not, we need to grasp the Hebrew poetry of the narrative, which flows around a female/male rhythm.

First, when the narrative speaks of humanity being taken from the earth, the word for humanity is *adam*, while the word for the earth from which humanity is taken is *adamah*. In terms of gender, the *adam* is male while the *adamah* is female. Thus symbolically the emergence of humanity from the earth is the emergence of the male from the female.

If we approach this imagery not through the classical or modern imagination, which sees the lower as inferior, but rather through the primal imagination which tended to see the divine revelation of life as coming from below, through the religious and life-giving mystery of the "earth mother," then the emergence of the *adam* from the *adamah* might be seen as the emergence of human life from the divinely rooted creativity of the earth mother. Rather than stressing the male principle as superior (meaning higher), this narrative may in fact be stressing the female principle as the immediate source of life, or in other words the rootedness of the human in the maternal creativity of the ecological.

A confirmation that we tend to see these Genesis narratives through the classical and modern imaginations, rather than through the primal imagination out of which they arose, is the fact that the event of sin is commonly described as "the fall." Yet the book of Genesis nowhere uses the term "fall." This is a projection of the classical transcendent model, based on the classical Greek vision of the great chain of being, where the higher is holy and the lower is less worthy. But the projection obscures the meaning of the myth.

For the primal consciousness, falling would mean not falling into sin, but rather falling back into the arms of the female side of the Creator, revealed through the life-death cycles of the earth mother.

By contrast, for Genesis the sin event might better be described not as a fall, but as a rise, that is the attempt to rise out of or escape from the creative communion of ecological-social-spiritual intimacy. Recall that the Genesis narrative of sin climaxes in the pride-filled erection of the tower of Babel. Quite perceptively in the Christian tradition, the antidote to the rising sin of pride is humility, that is awareness of our rootedness in the *humus*, namely the earth. Falling into earthiness is the redemptive healing of ascendant pride.

Second, although the woman is taken from the body of the man, here again there is a rhythmic poetry. The Hebrew word for man is *is* and the Hebrew word for woman is *issah*. Thus the overall rhythm across the two narratives is reciprocal and non-hierarchical. In the first narrative, the *adamah* yields the *adam*, while in the second narrative the *is* yields the *issah*. In other words, female yields male and then male yields female. The image is not hierarchical, but circular, as indeed was the imagination of the primal stage.

What do we learn then of human work from a primal view of the two Genesis narratives of creation? First, that work in God's original creation was to be understood as the cherishing and caring process of an ecological-social-spiritual garden. Second, that sexuality is intimately linked to the work process, with its symbolism disclosing the female and male dimensions of the divine revelation, as well as the circular complementarity of society and ecology in the work process.

Of course this circular ecological-social-spiritual holism, reflected in the mutuality and circularity of the female-male symbols, is shattered by the event of sin. But what is the meaning of this sin, and what is the meaning of its healing?

3. The Sin Narrative

The unfolding story of sin begins with Genesis 3:1 and continues up to its challenge in the rainbow covenant with Noah (a covenant with all living things of the earth) in Genesis 9 and the call of Abram in Genesis 12.

The unfolding of sin begins with an event linked with knowledge and sexuality. Some have interpreted this event as sexual awakening, but that cannot be the case since the command to be fruitful and multiply precedes the event of sin. Rather the sin must be not in the fact of sexual awakening, but in the manner in which it came to human consciousness.

Note that the sin event is tied to the human attempt to gain divine control over life. Hence it may be the use of sexuality for manipulative control rather than creative communion which is the sin.

Often the sin event is blamed on woman, but that overlooks the fact that in the symbolic imagination the serpent is often a phallic symbol, often used as a representative of male sexuality in fertility cults. Popular folklore links the serpent with the devil, and that may indeed be a legitimate expansion of the myth. But there is no mention of the devil within the narrative. Thus, from within the primal consciousness, we might view the sin event as beginning with the male symbol (the serpent), seducing the female symbol (Eve), and passed on again from woman to man (Adam)—in effect a circular process.

The whole narrative of the creation of woman and the seduction of woman may be a polemic against the classical Middle Eastern ritual of temple prostitution, which attempted to use sexuality as a manipulative tool for social and ecological control. The sin is to degrade the intimate sexual communion in its most personalistic depths, and thus to unleash a shattering process across the ecological-social-spiritual whole of creation. But the sin would not be sexuality. It would be the desire for domineering control rather than creative communion. The first sin is thus the first expression of human violence.

As Genesis then tells us, this violence in the most intimate and personal process of sexuality constantly works its way outward to wider ecological-social-spiritual alienation. Let us look now at each of these alienations.

In the spiritual alienation, humanity begins to hide from God, who in turn becomes transcendently remote and accessible only through the destructive act of sacrifice by an increasingly separated priesthood. Intimacy with the divine is now blocked, as a great gulf separates the divine and the human, with the divine apparently appeased only by destruction of some element of creation. And, as we know from history, the priesthood is conceived socially in hierarchical terms, that is as a higher class, and sexually in male terms, that is as the dominating gender. In this process the female and earthly-mediated image of God, so powerfully communicated in the first creation narrative as half of the revelation of the divine image, now recedes before an expanding male transcendent image of the divine.

In the social alienation, society becomes increasingly hierarchical, fragmented, and murderous. The first sin, limited to the realm of personal intimacy, becomes in the next generation the murder of Abel by his brother Cain.

Cain and his descendants are in turn linked with the early metal revolution—the early use of iron, copper, and bronze, and eventually (growing out of early metal technologies) the construction of the first cities. The very name Cain means blacksmith, and the first major development of weapons (as well as of tools in general) comes from the manipulation of metal by early smiths.

As technology develops, so too grows the technological implications of sin. Cain's great-great-great grandson Tubal-Cain is named as the forger of implements of copper and iron. And just as violence against Cain was to be avenged sevenfold, so violence against Lamech, the father of Tubal-Cain, was to be avenged seventy-sevenfold. As the metallurgical technology grows, so grows the scale of violence.

Cain is also named as the founder of a city, the first mentioned in the Bible, and now technologically possible because of metal instruments to carve stone and to conquer peoples. The ancient city thus was built on social violence—through forced labor in its very construction and in turn acting as a strategic fortress for aristocratic domination of the surrounding peasantry.

In addition to this class violence, sexual violence became institutionalized with the rise of civilization. Patriarchy became the model both for the sphere of intimacy and for wider social structures. Thus Genesis tells us that now the man shall rule over the woman (Chapter 3, verse 16). Similarly, the aristocratic classes of the city were uprooted from the *adamah* of the earth, and in turn control the peasantry whose life is bound up with intimacy with the *adamah*. The fact of rule by one over another is thus not something natural to humanity, but a consequence of sin.

As male rules female, so aristocrat rules peasant. Thus the uprooted male symbol itself became increasingly linked with violence and transcendence. Sexual domination and class domination become micro and macro of sin's consequences.

Finally, this spiritual and social alienation was inextricably linked to ecological alienation. The work process became a place of harsh struggle, no longer a garden, but now a terrain bristling with thorns and thistles, dealt with only by the sweat of the brow. Similarly the sexual process, the psychological root of the work process, becomes a place of alienation where harmony is gone and child-bearing comes only through pain.

What does this all tell us then of work? First that work, as humanity's creative communion with life's ecological-social-spiritual whole, lost its harmony through sin. Second, that this loss of harmony brought alienation and fragmentation into our ecological, social, and spiritual relationships, including in the sexual-social terrain the related emergence of patriarchal domination and violence. Third, that as the technological processes of humanity's work develop, so too develops the scale of sin's destructiveness.

The Consequent Historical Development of Work

In the human journey since its primal origins, the work process has passed through two major structural shifts, the agricultural revolution and the industrial revolution. Now it seems to be entering a third phase.[18]

1. Three Revolutions in Work

The first shift was from the work style of a society of food gatherers to a society based on the care of animals and crops.

It began ten to eleven thousand years ago, leading perhaps six thousand years ago to the first cities, presumably in the Middle East.

This shift led over time to the creation of large, urban-centered priestly and military empires based on the religious and military control of massive river-based agricultural systems which relied upon the aristocratic centers for their irrigation system. The first of these empires arose in the Mesopotamian river plains—first the Sumerian, then the Babylonian, then the Assyrian, and finally the Persian empires. The controlling center was originally the temple, functioning as a major landowner and a political and economic as well as religious center. Later, however, by the third millennium B.C., the palace had been separated from the temple and began to rival it. It was on this Middle Eastern imperial legacy that the west built its classical civilization.[19] The system of work of these classical empires was often based on slave labor, or serfdom, set over against a hierarchical elite which transcended the earthy side of the work process.

The second major shift of the industrial revolution, which began only a few hundred years ago, linked human labor with powerful machines, but also began to plunder the earth and to turn workers into instruments of machines and bureaucracies.

Yet both these shifts in the work process enormously advanced humanity's scientific-technological capacity and laid the foundation for a truly mature human project now emerging in the third revolution of work.

The third shift in the work process is only now beginning. We call this the birth of an information society, post-industrial in character. But let us hold off speaking of this new social form and instead review how the prior two revolutions both technologically advanced and simultaneously began to degrade the work process, resulting in the late modern context in a fundamental threat on life.

2. *The Contradiction of Progress*

Again, in its hypothetical primal state humanity had been at one with nature, at one with itself, and at one with God. But this primal holism was still childlike, for it had not yet discovered its own creative power. It simply stood in communing awe with the creative energy of the divine source and its surrounding natural garden.

When humanity took its first steps toward techno-scientific maturity, it opened the door to creativity in the work process, but also planted violence at its heart. The unfolding of humanity's co-creative energy emerged only by means of, or accompanied by, a threefold violence: (1) the plunder of nature; (2) the exploitation of labor; (3) religious alienation.

a. The *religious violence* was to try to define humanity's creative powers as spiritually autonomous, that is as independent of their divine source. This was the violence of pride, which becomes the root of all other violence. Thus the children of the garden, once they tasted the fruit of the tree of knowledge, tried to hide from the Creator.

In ancient times, this hiding from God took expression in the separation of the sacred and the profane. (The profane means "outside the temple," suggesting that the sacred was limited to the temple.) God would no longer be celebrated within the creative process of work. Rather the tendency was to identify the divine only with the experience of transcendence. Thus secular work became profane, and hence unholy. Later, with the rise of modern scientific-technological culture, the divine would be excluded from public life entirely, even its transcendent dimension.

b. The *social violence* was to exploit human labor. The work process was scarred by fundamental and antagonistic divisions, based on class, sex, race, and geography. These divisions were the many oppressions which came to mark human labor—the patriarchal domination of men over women, the class domination of masters over slaves, lords over serfs, and capital over labor, the racial domination of lighter skinned peoples over darker skinned peoples, and the geographic domination of colonizing centers over colonized peripheries.

Further, in the modern context, the work process was increasingly polarized and atomized so that the human community began to erode.

Again, this social oppression in work was the organizational basis of the earliest cities and of classical civilizations. The few rose above the many by controlling irrigation and the surplus of agricultural production, thus making possible the creation of political, military, and religious elites. The city in turn was made possible by technological advances in metallurgy, whose tools were the basis of more productive agriculture and grandiose architecture, and whose weapons were the basis of social domination.

The modern form of the work process gradually undermined many of these classical oppressions. Instead it strove to substitute egalitarian relationships among all workers, no matter their sex, race, or religion. But the homogeneity for which modern work strove also produced a new oppression based on a common instrumentalization of labor. Workers became expendable instruments of giant corporations or state bureaucracies, in effect the tools of a giant social machine.

c. The *ecological violence*, perhaps the most fundamental, was again the alienation from nature. In this violence human elites tried to break their organic ties with the wider ecology. Humanity is the most creative revelation of the earth's evolutionary drive. But paradoxically humanity turned against the earth which bore it.

3. *The Roots of the Modern in the Classical*

In classical societies, the exercise of creative consciousness was limited to aristocratic elites, including political, military, and religious elites. These elites developed an ideology of hierarchy, by which they understood the human elite as totally transcending nature. Their highest energies were directed to escape from nature through the contemplation of eternal essences uprooted from the particular limits of time and space. The contemplative cultural vision was in turn embodied in classical art forms.

The systems of economic domination established by these elites saw economic activity as part of a lower material realm, useful only to provide a platform for launching transcendent activities like philosophy, contemplation, friendship, and politics. In this process the holy was defined as transcendent, beyond the cycles of nature.

The classical spiritual flight from the earth enabled modernity to subject the earth to modern manipulative experiment. Hence it is a mistake to think that the modern loss of spirituality is simply a consequence of forgetfulness of our classical religious roots. Rather it is partly a consequence of the alienated and uprooted religious consciousness of classicism itself. Secular modernity is classicism's technological follow-through.

This modern loss of reverence, even for transcendence, leads to a form of development which eventually threatens all life on the planet. Cain's sevenfold violence, and Lamech's seventy-sevenfold multiplication of Cain's violence are but petty vibrations in human history, compared to the destructive possibility of late modern civilization.

As the scale of sin's power increased each time with technological development, so now in late modern culture for the first time in human history alienated humanity has the power to destroy all life of earth. What even God refused to do in the flood now becomes technologically feasible for an autonomous and uprooted techno-scientific civilization.

In times past the human destruction of vast regions of

ecology, or massacre of vast populations of society, was but a temporary setback, inevitably overcome by life's ecological and social capacity to rebound. The crisis of late modern culture, and hence fundamentally the crisis of its work process, is that there is now in place the technological capacity to inflict a fatal wound on the entire ecological-social system, a wound from which we would never recover.

In other words, the productive system now has the capacity (and to many, it seems, the intention) to destroy the reproductive system. It is this most fundamental crisis that the deepest levels of all ecological-social-spiritual struggles are really about—from contaminated oceans to contaminated food, from nuclear war to abortion, from religious authoritarianism to privatized pietism. Technological development has reached a scale where the power of sin could be terminal.

Yet I do not believe that need be the case. In order to make it not the case, we need to face up to the depths of the crisis. To find a path of healing, let us turn from the sin event to the Jesus event.

Jesus as the New Creation

Jesus' gospel speaks to the work process not because he grew up in a carpenter's family, but because he proclaims a new creation. At the most fundamental level, this means a healing and re-creation of the work process. Of course, ultimately Christians believe this healing will find only eschatological fulfillment. But we also believe that the healing process is active right now in human history. So, unless the late modern crisis is in fact the edge of the eschaton (certainly a possibility but not one we are allowed to presume), then we must search for how the Christian presence in the world can reorient the work process away from its potentially lethal course.

I propose that, as with Genesis, we begin with the point

where sin apparently began—the spiritual relationship with the Creator as mediated through the experience of sexuality in marriage and family. I will further propose that, in order to heal the destructiveness of late modern culture, Christianity is called to help rediscover the primal consciousness of ecological-social-spiritual holism and to integrate it with the post-modern micro-electronic technological revolution. But before turning to how this might play itself out in post-modern culture, let us recall a few dimensions of Jesus' healing gospel which may guide us in the new situation.

1. The Overcoming of Sexual Violence

First, as we read in Mark 10:2–12, Jesus' new creation promises to restore the primal nature of sexuality in the male/female relationship as it was before the sin event. In reply to a question about Moses' permitting divorce, Jesus answers that it was permitted "because of stubbornness," that is because of the condition of sin. But he then returns to the creation narrative of Genesis, repeating that *In the beginning God made them male and female; for this reason a man shall leave his father and mother and the two shall become as one. They are no longer two but one flesh. . . .*

Often it is the tendency to read this statement of Jesus legalistically, as if under the Mosaic law divorce was permitted to Jews, but under the Christian law it is not permitted. That may be the consequence, but the meaning of the statement is richer.

Jesus is telling us that entering into the covenant with him, we actually return to the primal condition before sin and its consequences. This means not simply that divorce is forbidden, but more profoundly that marriage, and within it sexuality, can be healed from the sexual violence which has cursed history since the sin event. This also means that in the Christian experience patriarchy (where man rules over woman) is to be no more, for patriarchy was a consequence of sin. It means too that fertile and communing sexuality is the starting point for the healing of the work process.

2. *The Overcoming of Institutional Violence*

Just as personal sexual violence was the root of institutional social violence after the sin event, so Jesus' healing of personal sexuality by a return to the creation model of marriage is accompanied by a return to the holistic sense of social community found before the sin event. Thus, in Matthew 20:25 we read,

> *You know how those who exercise authority among the Gentiles lord it over them; their great ones make their importance felt. It cannot be so like that with you.*

Again, Jesus is not giving a legalistic command for personal self-effacement, but proclaiming a new possibility within his re-creation, that is within his restoration of conditions in creation before the sin event. Hence, Jesus is proclaiming a model for social institutions, at least for the institutions of his faith community, which would be free of the class domination of Roman imperialism—for the powerful Gentiles of his context were the Romans.

In this rejection of "lording over," Jesus holds up the primal symbol of the child as the model for social organization. Again all the values are inverted—the first become last, the last first; the great are small, the small great; the powerful weak, and the weak powerful; the poor blessed, the rich cursed; those who seek to secure their life will lose it, while those who are willing to risk death are reborn; and so on. Hence Jesus' model is not the classical model of domination. It is simply the holistic communion of the original creation.

3. The Healing Fall

Whoever would be first will be last. The temple will be destroyed. The son of man was buried in a tomb. All of these symbols speak of the redemptive humbling of the male symbol. The billions of expressions of ambition across history which sought to rise up above the rest, to rise away from nature, away from the common people, and away from the mystery of God revealed in ecological-social creation—all of these violent ambitions are suddenly rejected in the fall of Jesus on the cross.

Here is the true meaning of falling, not into sin, but into healing. Perhaps that is why we speak of falling in love. The healing comes precisely by rejecting the prideful and violent rise to power. Only after that, in the authentic and divine power of the Spirit, the same *ruah* that breathed over the waters of Genesis and over the waters of Exodus, only in that truly creative spirit can the defeated destructive pride of the alienated male symbol be healed.

The falling is healing because, contrary to the temptation of Genesis' phallic symbol of the snake and its later expansion in the tower of Babel, Jesus falls back to the tomb (a maternal symbol of the womb), back to the life-giving embrace of the *ruah*.

Hence in these three areas—sexuality as the intimate root of the life process, social organization as the institutional enlargement of that root, and the bi-polar meaning of the male and female symbols—Jesus proclaims to us the path to re-creation: sexuality as marriage's one flesh, creative, holistic, and non-patriarchal; institutional power as a child-like inversion, rejecting the imperial model of "rule over" and instead calling for a creative community of mutual service and leadership by the least; and, finally, the experience of falling as the path to healing by the earthy and female side of the divine image.

It is this gospel which carries the healing message for

modernity's destructive sin. It is this call which is to guide the Christian community as it turns to the healing and celebration of humanity's work. Now we can ask how this influences the post-modern creation of a holistic economy.

Seeds of a Post-Modern Holism

The post-modern economy, flowing from the third revolution in the human work process, is based on an intensified network of communications and transportation. This network is made possible by the microelectronic technology, that is, by the miniaturization of electronic circuits. Again, we refer to this form of society now being born as an information society. The control of information becomes the basis of post-modern social institutions, much as the control of capital was the basis in the modern era and the control of land in the classical era.

The creative challenge for post-modern society is to direct the work process toward non-violence, healing the wounds caused by the threefold violence of past stages of human culture. Specifically this challenge is (1) to reintegrate human work within the ecological rhythm, (2) to recover the priority and solidarity of labor, all within the building up of human community, and (3) to rediscover the profound spiritual meaning of human work. If this happens, then to some degree the post-modern economy may redirect the Faustian energies of modernity.

Presently only the seeds of a creative post-modern work process are to be found. But these seeds carry the promise of a new stage of human culture and of an historical reshaping of work around the creativity of ecological, social, spiritual communion. It is important to recognize these seeds, protect them from threats, and nurture their growth into the future.

1. Spiritual Seeds

Gratefully the Catholic tradition is turning its spiritual energies back to embrace the world. This accounts for the central role in the Second Vatican Council (1962–1965) of the document entitled *Gaudium et Spes (Pastoral Constitution on the Church in the Modern World)*. Earlier than Vatican II, José María Escriva, founder of *Opus Dei*, articulated the beginnings of a lay spirituality centered in human work. Similarly, in the wake of Vatican II, Latin American liberation theology found spiritual meaning in the social struggle for justice by the poor in the periphery of industrial capitalism. Likewise an older liberation theology, namely black American Christianity, revealed the spiritual strength that flowed from the oppressed work of slaves. Also new feminist spiritualities, reacting against the hierarchical dualisms of male theologies, explore a holistic spirituality of creative embodiment. The recent stream of creation-centered spirituality, integrating the primal immanent spirituality with mystical insights flowing from post-modern science, reveals the deep creativity of the universe. Finally, Pope John Paul II, in his speeches and writings, and especially in *Laborem Exercens*, has focused Catholic social thought on the co-creativity of work, articulated in the principle of the priority and solidarity of human labor and the framework of global human community.

All these examples suggest a powerful and fundamental reversal of the uprooted spiritualities of the high classical consciousness, as well as a break beyond the destructive fragmentation of the modern consciousness. Indeed, taken as a whole, these examples point toward a post-modern integration of spiritual and scientific consciousness, in turn shaping holistically the post-modern work process.

While in most cases it will be too early to expect major post-modern transformations in the objective structures of work, namely in the organization of labor and in the form of technology, we can begin with this transformation of our religious consciousness of work. We can try to discover in our own work and in the work of others our share in the divinely driven creativity of the universe. We can then celebrate the religious mystery of human work in our personal and communal prayer.

If we begin to do this, it may not be long before our eyes are opened wide to the modern degradation of work, and to the post-modern possibilities. We may find ourselves compelled by our spiritual energy to press for holistic structural ways of organizing labor and shaping technology.

2. *Social Seeds*

As we have already explored, both modern capitalism and modern communism (or anything in between) fail to provide an adequate ecological, social, or spiritual vision to lead us beyond the modern crisis. Rather we need a fresh vision of the social dimension of the work process, that is in the relationship among workers (the organization of labor). The key principle here is again the communal creativity of human labor.

This principle is being explored by new experiments in cooperative, rather than competitive economics. While there are many cooperative experiments underway in the mainstream capitalist and communist worlds, the most dramatic experiments come from outside these ideological streams in two movements, first what has been called "economic democracy," and second what has been called "appropriate technology."[20]

a. *Economic democracy* means pioneering new forms of worker participation, from the most extensive form of a renewal of the cooperative movement to lesser forms of worker cooperation in mixed or privately held companies. One of the best known examples is the network of cooperatives in the Basque country in the north of Spain.

These are known as the Mondragon Group. They grew

out of the initiatives of a local parish priest, José María Arizmendi Arriéta, who encouraged unemployed youth to undertake technical training and to start their own factory. Eventually the movement grew into a vast complex of industrial cooperatives, a central cooperative bank, a research and development institute, and a cooperative university. Today workers own the factories where they work and many young workers spend half the day in their factory and the other half in the university, which they also own. In this model, management does not hire labor, but labor hires management, thus affirming the principle of the priority of labor.

While the Mondragon Group is not perfect, it is one powerful example that we can now structure our economy in a different way. The meaning of this cooperative model needs to be explored at every level, from the local, to the regional, to the national, to the global.[21]

b. *Appropriate technology* refers to technology that is artistically shaped to promote cooperation among workers, and also cooperation between workers and nature. Thus it has both a social and an ecological dimension.

We tend to think of technology as having a single trajectory where progress can follow only one inevitable course. But technology can be shaped any number of ways, depending on the values which are brought to the shaping process. For example a society centered on solar energy would be very different than a society centered on nuclear energy.[22]

Much of modern technology has been aimed at supporting the concentration of power in large transnational corporations or state bureaucracies, as well as at the mass control of workers and citizens. Now we need to learn how to shape technology in the service of the priority and solidarity of labor, in turn centered in the support of global/local human community. This means first of all using technology in service of labor, and not the reverse. It also means, where feasible, developing small-scale technology that workers can own and control. Again, the micro-electronic revolution in technology facilitates this possibility.

3. Ecological Seeds

The ecological side of the post-modern form of work will be the fruit of the post-modern scientific vision. The modern scientific vision, rooted especially in Newtonian physics, saw nature as an inert, fragmented, random field of forces open to extrinsic manipulation by the objective use of technical controls. But new insights coming from the frontiers of post-modern physics, especially astro and sub-atomic physics, no longer accept this cosmology. Rather they propose that the universe is a communal, creative whole, even mystical in character, and that we humans find our identity first within our ecological roots. Hence we need to redefine work from the classical and modern frameworks of mastering and manipulating nature from above or outside to a post-modern framework of cooperating with nature's own creativity from within.[23]

Taken together these three seeds—ecological, social, spiritual—constitute the conceptual foundations of a post-modern restructuring of work. It now remains for us to ask how communities of Christians can assist in giving birth to this new cultural expression of the work process. That is the subject of the next and final chapter.

Summary

This chapter has explored the proposal that the future of work and civilization is linked not so much to the on-going debate between classical and modern views, but rather to the linkage of pre-classical primal memories of holism and of the techno-scientific possibilities of the post-modern imagination. This link in turn was traced to the primal vision of Genesis and to Jesus' re-creation of the Genesis vision. Finally it explored some spiritual, social, and ecological seeds of the post-modern vision of work.

4.
Post-Modern Pastoral Implications

In this fourth chapter I would like to ask the important question of what all this means for the pastoral life of the contemporary church. I will not propose a full strategy for the post-modern church, but only suggest some leading strategic issues for the church in the transition from a modern to a post-modern pastoral orientation.

In asking this question I would like to address a small selection of themes to illustrate the proposed pastoral orientation: (1) a general pastoral consciousness regarding work; (2) the shifting work roles of women and men, and the consequent new model of family; (3) the special problem of unemployment and the possibility of the church's planting seeds of a post-modern development model; (4) the fresh challenge to unions. This is only a partial list of pastoral concerns, but hopefully these themes will stimulate the post-modern pastoral imagination.

Pastoral Consciousness of Work

The starting point for a post-modern pastoral strategy, which deals seriously with work, is consciousness of work's religious depth. This sounds simple, but there is little evidence of its presence. There are perhaps two reasons for absence of concern with work in most pastoral efforts.

The first reason comes from church professionals. As mentioned, classical and modern spiritualities (largely supported in the past by church professionals) considered as religious only work directly for the religious institution. All other work was seen as lacking a "religious vocation."

The second reason comes from the nature of work in modern industrial society. Prior to the industrial revolution, the production and reproduction processes were closely connected. Most work was still within the family, for example family farms or small family businesses. But the industrial revolution began a long and deepening process of separating production from reproduction, and hence work from family. Later, with the modern automobile and the consequent growth of residential communities separate from areas of production, the physical distance between family and work often became enormous.

Meanwhile the church established its modern pastoral system mostly in reference to the residential patterns, without reference to workplaces. Thus modern pastoral agents normally minister to people on the consumer side of their lives, or only with the reproductive work of housewives, parents, and spouses. The productive side of work has been generally left out of pastoral consciousness, and out of pastoral strategy.

This happened quite unintentionally. Five hundred years ago, when the parish priest walked down the middle of the small European village, with the parish church at its center, he walked through the world of family and work. Today, however, the parish is isolated on the consumer side, and the priest perhaps touches the world of family (though even this is now eroding) but scarcely touches the world of work.

A great danger, I fear, in the American turn to small Christian communities (important as they are) is that these faith communities will simply reinforce this productive/reproductive split. Such small communities could easily take shape as what the religious sociologist Robert Bellah has called "life-style enclaves," disconnected from the public work of society.[24]

This danger was confirmed for me in a recent review of some thirty articles proposed by a range of writers for an American Catholic newspaper on small faith communities. The proposed topics addressed exclusively a series of four important themes, namely the self, the family, the parish, and the local community. But all of these themes are confined to the realm of subjective intimacy, around which the modern pastoral strategy has been constructed. They prescinded entirely from the techno-scientific world of work. There was no mention of business, commerce, government, law, medicine, engineering, accounting, military, diplomacy, etc. These work areas are largely beyond the modern pastoral and spiritual consciousness.

In much of Europe this spiritual isolation in consuming subjectivity led to the de-Christianization of large sectors of the working class. Because the European church generally failed to address the religious dimension of the productive experience of the working classes, European industrial workers often failed to find in the faith community a place to celebrate and probe their spiritual experience of work. Instead they often found it in the scientistic religion of Marxism.

Fortunately in the United States we did not initially suffer this loss of the working class. This was partly because here the church did support workers' struggles, and more likely because the old rural peasant patterns (from which so many immigrant workers came) temporarily survived as defensive ethnic ghettos in a new and hostile industrial society. But this pattern may not persist in the "post-immigrant" phase of Euro-American Catholicism, especially when large numbers of women are also being drawn into the paid labor force.

The danger of creating life-style enclaves in the name of

small faith communities is accentuated by the new middle class character of the Euro-American wing of American Catholicism. The middle classes are more easily socialized into the modern fragmented consciousness of multiple specializations, and hence more easily separate religion from their work. Hence, different than the working classes, they more easily maintain an active church life on the consumer side, yet keep it separate from the wider world of economics and politics. Hence while the European working classes tended toward abandonment of religious practice, the new American middle classes tend toward privatization of religion. With few exceptions, the pastoral strategy of American Catholicism accepts this model.

But what would it mean to reintegrate work outside the home back into pastoral strategy, that is to relink production with reproduction in the religious consciousness and pastoral strategy?[25]

One place to begin would be liturgy and preaching. The religious celebration on Sunday should be the place where we celebrate the religious meaning of life during the week, including work outside the home. It should also be a place which provides prophetic challenge to any degradation of work's religious meaning. Unfortunately, the work experience is generally excluded from liturgical-pastoral life. We need to find practical ways of bringing the experience of work into the center of preaching, liturgy, and the whole pastoral strategy. At the very least we need to remember the religious depth of work and to understand its contemporary forms.

This would mean, I should think, that pastoral agents would visit the workplaces of their community members, just as, hopefully, they visit their homes. They would discuss the work experience with these members, and provide more structured ways for reflecting evangelically on the work process. If pastoral agents were to take this task seriously, it probably would not be long before the liturgy and preaching, indeed all their pastoral work, would embrace the fundamental religious experience of human work.

Female/Male Roles and a Partnership Model of Family

A second major concern for pastoral agents is the changing work roles of women and men, and their consequent impact on the family.

By and large the pastoral strategy of most modern parishes has been built around the experience of the modern family, in turn based on three social principles. First, most men normally worked away from the home and even from the geographic area of the parish, while most women remained within it. Second, the nurture of children within the family was largely the concern of their mothers, since the fathers were at such a distance. Third, the family structure was patriarchal with the father seen as the ultimate head, although the mother functioned as a more immediate authority for the children with the father as a back-up.

In turn the modern parish generally presumed these three principles in its pastoral strategy. First the parish, like the family, was largely sustained by the voluntary work of women who remained in the residential community. Second, in and through these women, and women who committed themselves to a "religious vocation," the parish dealt with the religious education of the children. Third, the parish followed the same patriarchal model of family in its modern adaptation, that is with the clergy acting as the more remote father-like authority figures (actually called "father") and the women (mothers, sisters, and single female volunteers) religiously socializing the children.

Now this pastoral model, like the social model on which it was founded, is breaking down. Women are rapidly drawn into paid labor outside the home. Sisters are removing themselves from the school apostolate, partly because of declining numbers, partly because of other interests. Men are slowly taking on partnership roles with women in marriage, in parenting, and in general social life. In the industrial capitalist world clerical life draws fewer candidates, and experiences serious internal losses. The family itself, like the wider community, comes under new and enormous strains, leading to epidemic levels of divorce, single parent families, and abortion. And in the TV era, a parish-centered system of religious socialization, uprooted from the family, seems to have declining influence.

The deep structural reason for all these changes is that society's traditional system of social and biological reproduction is now being invaded and displaced by the expanding technological power of the modern production system. Until recently the modern work process was founded on a limited technological basis, which enabled family, community, and parish to remain relatively insulated from the great changes occurring in the apparently external work process. But with the late modern explosion of transportation and communications, especially the proliferation of the automobile and television, the family, community, and parish are no longer insulated. They are dramatically impacted by the erosion of ecological, social, and spiritual communion stemming from the modern degradation of work.

In this modern erosion of ecological, social, and spiritual reproduction, the value system of modern technological work begins to undermine family and community life (the natural social foundation of parish life). At the same time the shifting roles of women and men gradually strip religious meaning from traditional spiritualities which are based on the division of male and female symbols into segregated and hierarchically ordered productive and reproductive spheres.

There are three distinct strategic paths for responding to this challenge.

One strategic path is to accept the modernization process as inevitable and perhaps positive, and to live reluctantly with the ensuing breakdown of family and community—doing one's best to minister to the victims. The second strategic path is to react negatively against the modern breakdown, and to attempt to preserve by authoritarian means the decaying pre-modern patriarchal family model, perhaps in a traditionalist ghetto, and to legitimate its wider social echoes.

The third strategic path is to reach beyond the modernization process itself, openly accepting its gifts but boldly challenging its degradation, in order to create some fresh postmodern model of family based on male/female partnership in the productive and reproductive spheres, and to attempt to extend this model to all social institutions.

There are of course lessons to be learned from all three strategies, but I believe only the third can provide a fundamental pastoral guide for our new context.

Accepting this third strategy would mean achieving a new synthesis or partnership between the functions of production and reproduction, that is a whole new definition of work. This in turn leads to a new pattern of male and female roles, where both jointly share in the two worlds, with women now entering the history-shaping productive world of the paid labor market and men recovering their biological roots in the reproductive world of family and community.

This would not mean that women and men simply change places (the conservative fear), nor that women become assimilated to an uprooted male model (the liberal tendency), but rather that both would join in a fresh partnership in both spheres. This would lead to a female-male partnership model for family and work, and for church as well.

Yet full female-male partnership in a holistic integration of the productive and reproductive dimensions of work is not the path which the modernization process pursues. The gift of modernization has been to expose the injustice of the traditional pattern of male domination over the female. But its evil has been to seek only to democratize the female into the uprooted male world, and thus to allow production to erode reproduction. Again partnership in both spheres would lead to a post-modern vision of work, where production and reproduction holistically become two dimensions of all work.

What would this third, post-modern vision mean for pastoral strategy? It would mean religiously celebrating the new partnership model of family, the new holism in female/male role models across family, work, and church, as well as the integration of the productive and reproductive dimensions of life and its religiously symbolic expression. It would mean finding new ways for ministering to both spouses in the work of family and paid employment. It would mean calling for new social patterns, especially a shortened work week (of paid work outside the home), so that both spouses would have more time for each other, for children, for politics, for community, and for parish. It would mean giving high priority to a linked family and work ministry, including perhaps a full time family/work counselor on a parish staff.

The great danger of the present modern pastoral strategy, however, is that it might not accept this post-modern vision. Instead it could simply continue its present course without challenge to the trajectory of modernization, thus threatening the loss to the church of the new generation of female workers as well as of whole families based on the new model. In reaction, a traditionalist strategy would try to organize the small number of women not working outside the home against the new post-modern roles for women and men.

But, I believe, neither of these two strategies, the modern nor the traditionalist, will prove adequate. Both will accelerate the ecclesial and social crisis.

Unemployment and Alternative Development

One major pastoral concern is unemployment. The late modern stage of industrial society appears to be marginalizing a large proportion of the labor force into a permanent underclass of structurally unemployed. Technology, following only the logic of modernity, begins to displace labor. This is especially true on a world scale where a global crisis of unemployment grows deeper. There is little evidence that the free market or the state will provide authentic work for this global permanent underclass.

Unemployment is a religious degradation. It denies the vocation of the unemployed to be co-creators through the work process with God, nature, and the rest of society. To be faithful to its religious vision, the church needs above all to challenge unemployment. Perhaps it can even create jobs which provide seeds of a post-modern model of economic development (based on the communal creativity, ecological rootedness, and the religious depth of work).

Hence the church could sponsor new employment-generating projects giving the unemployed a place to exercise their creativity through work. Such projects might be financed by capital loaned from the Christian community and embodied especially in cooperatives using appropriate technology to produce peaceful, socially needed, and ecologically responsible goods. Indeed such experiments are already beginning in the United States through the Campaign for Human Development, but the model might be taken more seriously.

It seems foreign to us to imagine the church as an employment-generator, but there is ample precedent in history. For example, early Celtic monasticism (in contrast to the Roman model of monasticism) did not separate itself from the wider community. Even the model of Roman monasticism later provided economic centers from which whole European cities and industries grew. For example, I remember once visiting a monastery in the English Midlands which during the late Middle Ages provided hundreds of jobs for local residents in the wool industry. Out of those monastic roots, the textile industry in that region probably grew.

But short of such an ambitious project, pastoral agents can begin an immediate ministry to the unemployed, especially to their spiritual needs. To suffer unemployment is not only a financial crisis, but also a devastating spiritual trauma. It often strips people of their deepest dignity, for they are denied space to exercise their creativity through work. Hence the unemployed need great spiritual affirmation. Prayer groups, counseling sessions, short-term financial assistance, community support—all of these are important pastoral needs of the unemployed.

The New Stage of Labor Organizations

In late modern industrial society there is a growing prejudice against unions. This is true in both capitalist and communist societies, as we now see a worldwide attack on labor which crosses ideological boundaries. It is a strategic attack on labor and its organization into unions.

In the third world of the developing countries of Africa, Asia, and Latin America, when workers try to organize to demand their rights they are often met with machine guns, torture, and execution by death squads. Were unions to grow strong in these places, transnational capital might not invest there because labor would no longer be cheap. The model for controlling third world labor is often the repressive national security dictatorship, as we have seen in Chile, South Africa, and the Philippines. Across the southern hemisphere unions are frequently waging a life and death struggle just to exist.

In the second world of the industrial communist nations

(the bloc dominated by the Soviet Union) protesting workers can be dealt with in more sanitary fashion. Where the state controls most of the jobs, one simple punishment is unemployment. If this is not sufficient, there may be need to confine the dissidents in a psychiatric institution, or finally in a remote prison camp or exile. For example, workers in Czechoslovakia who criticized Soviet deployment of SS-20 missiles were given an automatic ten year imprisonment. In a more serious case where workers begin to form their own authentic unions, as in Poland with *Solidarnosc*, there may be need for formal militarization of the state. Here again, the national security state becomes the model for the control of labor.

In the first world, the attack is more subtle but still pervasive. Unions are now seen as narrow-minded special interest groups opposed to the general progress of society. Management schools teach new anti-labor strategies. Collective bargaining is marked by "take-back" demands from management. New legislative initiatives are underway to curtail former pro-labor legislation. Unfortunately, even in the management policy of many American Catholic religious institutions, there are significant anti-labor patterns.

Across the first world, therefore, as well as in the third and second worlds, there is a clear strategic attack on the principle of workers' organizations.

If the labor movement is to deal creatively with this global attack, it will need to ask itself not simply how it can retreat into a fortress ghetto of defense, but rather how it can build on the new ecological, social, and spiritual vision of work arising with the birth of the post-modern era. In other words, how can the labor movement become a key bearer of the vision of ecological social and spiritual co-creativity.

This will mean, I propose, gradually displacing the dominance of the industrial model of unionism which characterized the labor movement in the middle years of this century.

The first stage of unionism in the industrial period was the dominance of *craft unionism*, rooted in the early entrepreneurial, localistic stage of the modern economy. Here the power of workers was based on their monopoly of skills and control over trade in a local market.

The second stage of unionism was the dominance of *industrial unionism*, rooted in the bureaucratic, nationalistic stage of the modern economy. Here the power of the workers was based on their mass political power, organized by large national trade union bureaucracies, and mediated through their impact on the social welfare state. It is the dominance of this second model which is now in cultural crisis, much as the dominance of the craft model went into crisis at the beginning of the century.

The new stage of the labor movement will be marked, I propose, by the following characteristics: a cooperative global/local approach to work, diminishing the role of the national structure and industrial divisions, an appropriation of the post-modern ecological, feminist, racial, and peace movements, and the formal public celebration of spiritual energy arising within the work process. In contrast to the craft and industrial styles, this post-modern style might be called *community unionism*, wherein the union becomes one of the key bearers of community at every level from the local to the global, and across the ecological, social, and spiritual axes.

Certainly there are only the faintest experiments in these areas, but in the meantime the post-modern pastoral strategy needs to affirm the abiding importance of workers' organizations, even while it critiques the failures of the diminishing industrial style.

Catholic social teaching has consistently upheld the right and importance of workers' organizing into unions. In his encyclical *Laborem Exercens*, Pope John Paul II calls unions an "indispensable" element of modern industrial life. Why this Catholic stress on the importance of unions?

From the viewpoint of contemporary Catholic social thought, where workers do not themselves own the means of production, unions are necessary in order that workers may have some decision-making power within the work process. Prior to industrial capitalism, when the production process was more simple, many workers were self-employed or protected by guilds. But the industrial revolution stripped many workers of the ownership of the means of production and their guilds. Hence a new institution was needed for their defense and also to participate in the decision-making process of work. Thus the emergence of modern unions.

The Catholic affirmation of unions is rooted in the theological nature of work wherein workers are not simply instruments of production to be hired and fired according to the laws of the market, nor simply to be scientifically managed without participation of their own organizations. Rather they are to make their voice felt in shaping the fundamental design of the work process. In an industrial system, where capital is largely controlled from outside the workers, be it by corporations or the state, workers need their organization into unions to realize the religious depth of their work.

Pastorally this would mean that the Christian community cannot be neutral on the principle of the rights of labor, any more than it can be neutral on the rights of the poor, the handicapped, the unborn, or anyone without a voice. Of course this does not mean that we need endorse every policy of unions, but we are called to defend their foundational rights. Support of workers' organizations in turn needs to be built into pastoral strategy, liturgical celebration, and preaching.

Summary

In this final summary, let us review the movement of the book as a whole across the four chapters.

In the first chapter, we saw how human work is being degraded by the mechanistic vision of modern civilization, be it capitalist or communist.

While modern capitalism has unfolded the divinely inspired technological imagination of the work process, it also often turns workers into exploited, manipulated, or expendable instruments of market-guided capital. This tends to make the free market a false god, and labor its instrument.

Modern communism tried to liberate labor from this degradation by having the state politically take over the market system. But communism keeps labor as its manipulated object, though this time instrumentalized by state-guided capital. This tends to make the state a false god and labor its instrument.

Hence the need not only for a more religious vision of work, but also for new structures of work to embody this religious vision.

The modern tendency to degrade human work threatens an ecological, social, and spiritual erosion of life's holistically creative communion. All life on earth is now threatened with destruction, rapidly by nuclear war or slowly by ecological contamination. Meanwhile the social fabric is being undermined, as we see in the crisis of family, the marginalization of unemployed labor, the general feelings of powerlessness and loneliness, and the decay of community. Finally society is becoming crassly despiritualized, losing its moral roots, with religion being pushed to the margin of privatization and replaced by a growing loss of meaning.

In the second chapter, we explored the deep religious meaning of work, namely that it is our share in humanity's communal creativity, arising from within the ecological creativity of the universe, and flowing ultimately from the creative love of the divine Creator. We saw how sin impacts work by degrading its religious meaning, and turning it from the path of social and ecological creativity. In response the overcoming of sin by grace heals work to restore its original creativity, and brings it to still greater religious depth.

Accepting this post-modern ecological-human-spiritual vision of work means moving beyond the often narrow and distorted understandings of work carried by certain strains of the western cultural tradition, for example the belief that work is a distraction from spirituality, that only church work is religious and the rest is secular, or that work is only a means to earn a living. Such distorted understandings of work from classical and modern spiritualities may be the ground out of which modern ideological degradation of work arose. Perhaps because "religious" people came to see the work of the world as outside the holy, the economy began over the long run to act as if it were indeed unholy, with destructive consequences.

To heal the destructiveness of modern industrial civilization, we need to allow the Spirit to unfold the vision that all human work is religious. Human work self-consciously realizes its religious meaning when it celebrates itself as the overflow of divine love, deepens its creative communion with its ecological source, and builds the human community.

In the third chapter we explored the question of how such a religious vision of work might be embodied in a post-modern civilization. The third chapter then suggested three moral principles for a post-modern embodiment of the religious vision of work, namely ecological co-creativity, human co-creativity, and divine co-creativity. Stated a different way, we may say that there are three principles informing the post-modern vision of work as creative communion: (1) its social framework, (2) its ecological rootedness, and (3) its religious depth. The third chapter then looked back to the primal symbolic memories as communicated to us by the book of Genesis, and linked them with the Jesus event as heralding a new creation overcoming ecological, social, and spiritual violence. Finally, this chapter linked these three principles with the world-embracing spirituality arising within Catholicism, with the two new economic movements of economic democracy and appropriate technology, and with the new post-modern ecologically-centered model of science.

This fourth chapter then proposed some pastoral implications of the post-modern spirituality of work: (1) a new pastoral consciousness of the religious dimension of work, (2) religious support for the new female/male partnership model of work and family, (3) church-based experiments in post-modern economic development empowering the unemployed, and (4) support for the principle of workers' organizations, especially in their post-modern experiments. Testing imaginative experiments in these areas could be at the heart of a post-modern pastoral strategy.

Notes

1. My earlier theological focus on the relationship of theology with political-economic theory and experience had two interests: (1) the exploration of a praxis model of theology where a social analysis of the political-economy became an important methodological moment, and (2) the articulation of a distinct analysis of three stages of industrial capitalism and, in response to this shifting political-economic context, of three Catholic strategies for evangelization. A brief summary of this material appeared in print in Chapter 4 of the book by Peter Henriot, S.J. and myself, *Social Analysis: Linking Faith and Justice* (2nd edition, Orbis Books/Center of Concern, Maryknoll, NY & Washington DC, 1980).

2. See Frijof Capra, *The Turning Point: Science, Society, and the Rising Culture* (New York: Bantam, 1982); Charlene Spretnak, *The Spirituality of Green Politics* (Santa Fe, New Mexico: Bear, 1986); Brian Swimme, *The Universe Is a Green Dragon: A Cosmic Creation Story* (Santa Fe, New Mexico: Bear, 1985); David Bohm, *Wholeness and Implicate Order* (New York: Ark, 1983); Anne Lonergan & Carole Richards, eds., *Thomas Berry and the New Cosmology* (Mystic, CT: Twenty-Third, 1987).

3. See various essays of mine in a forthcoming series of books on post-modernism, under the general editorship of David Griffin of the Center for a Postmodern World, to be published by the State University of New York Press.

4. See my Center of Concern Monograph, *The Post-Modern*

Cultural Earthquake: The Journey of Human Culture and the Current Conflict among Traditionalists, Modernists, and Post-Modernists (Washington DC: Center of Concern, 1985).

5. Gibson Winter, an Episcopalian theologian at Princeton University, has explored the cultural power of root metaphors in his important book *Liberating Creation: Foundations of Religious Social Ethics* (New York: Crossroad, 1981). I am indebted to him for opening this line of inquiry.

6. For more on the theoretical foundations of the modern interpretation of science, see again Capra, *The Turning Point,* especially Chapters 2 and 3.

7. For the official English version, see "Laborem Exercens," Third Encyclical of Pope John Paul II, *Origins,* NC Documentary Service, Vol. 11 (September 24, 1981), pp. 225–244.

8. See Robert A. Nisbet, *The Quest for Community* (New York: Oxford, 1953).

9. See Carolyn Merchant, *The Death of Nature: Women, Ecology, and the Scientific Revolution* (San Francisco: Harper & Row, 1983).

10. On this principle, see David Tracy, *The Analogical Imagination: Christian Theology and the Culture of Pluralism* (New York: Crossroad, 1981).

11. See for example Matthew Fox, *Original Blessing: A Primer in Creation Spirituality* (Santa Fe, New Mexico: Bear, 1983). For other names mentioned, see other references in these notes.

12. See Teilhard's essay, "The Formation of the Noosphere," in his collected essays, *The Future of Man* (New York: Harper & Row, 1964), pp. 161–191.

13. See Thomas Berry, *Riverdale Papers* (Riverdale, NY: Riverdale Center for Religious Research), the essay entitled "The Ecological Age" (no consistent pagination). Berry's terms for the four stages are: (1) the early tribal period, (2) the age of the great traditional civilizations, (3) the technological age, and (4) the ecological age.

14. See my essays in the forthcoming series mentioned earlier from the State University of New York press.

15. Again, the historian of science Carolyn Merchant, in her book *The Death of Nature: Women, Ecology, and the Scientific Revolution* (San Francisco: Harper & Row, 1980), has investigated how the technological explosion of the modern world was founded on this disparaging of nature.

16. The late E. F. Schumacher argued this case in his famous book, *Small Is Beautiful: Economics As If People Mattered* (New York: Harper & Row, 1973).

17. See Jurgen Moltmann, *God in Creation: A New Theology of Creation and the Spirit of God* (San Francisco: Harper & Row, 1985), pp. 29–31.

18. See Alvin Tofler, *The Third Wave* (New York: Bantam, 1981), and *Previews and Premises* (Boston: South End, 1984), as well as Clem Bezold, Rick J. Carlson, and Jonathan C. Peck, *The Future of Work and Health* (Dover, Mass.: Auburn House, 1986).

19. See Ruth Whitehouse and John Wilkins, *The Making of Civilization: History Rediscovered Through Archeology* (New York: Alfred A. Knopp, 1986).

20. See Martin Carnoy and Derek Shearer, *Economic Democracy: The Challenge of the Eighties* (Armonk, NY: M.E. Sharpe, 1980). The pioneering statements on appropriate technology are E.F. Schumacher's, *Small Is Beautiful* (New York: Harper & Row, 1973) and *Good Work* (New York: Harper & Row, 1980). For an overview of the experiments on Schumacher's ideas, see the book by his disciple George McRobie, *Small Is Possible* (New York: Harper & Row, 1981).

21. For more on Mondragon, see the Derek-Carnoy book cited above.

22. For more on appropriate technology, see the Schumacher references above.

23. For some initial experiments in this area, especially involving agriculture, see the work of the Regeneration Project, Emmaus, Pennsylvania. For reflections on the new scientific model, see the earlier reference.

24. See Robert Bellah, et al., *Habits of the Heart: Individualism and Commitment in American Life* (New York: Harper & Row, 1985).

25. An important resource for this task is the National Center for the Laity in Chicago. A key figure in this organization, Ed Marciniak, has stubbornly insisted on a spirituality of work, and in addition pioneered its exploration.